EARTHLY
PLEASURES

Also by Roger B. Swain
FIELD DAYS: JOURNAL OF AN ITINERANT BIOLOGIST

THE PRACTICAL GARDENER: A GUIDE TO
BREAKING NEW GROUND

SAVING GRACES: SOJOURNS OF A
BACKYARD BIOLOGIST

GROUNDWORK: A GARDENER'S ECOLOGY

EARTHLY

PLEASURES

TALES FROM A
BIOLOGIST'S GARDEN

ROGER B. SWAIN

Lyons & Burford, Publishers

To all who share
my fondness
for reading aloud

Printed in the United States of America
on recycled stock that includes 10% post-consumer waste.

10 9 8 7 6 5 4 3 2 1

All of the essays in this collection appeared originally in Horticulture. *The
cartoon on page 25 has been redrawn from* Punch, *volume 130, p. 53,
January 17, 1906, and has been used with permission.*

Library of Congress Cataloging-in-Publication Data

Swain, Roger B.
Earthly pleasures : tales from a biologist's garden / Roger B. Swain ;
illustrations by Laszlo Kubinyi.
p.   cm.
Originally published: New York : Scribner, 1981.
Includes bibliographical reference and index.
ISBN 1-55821-321-X
1. Gardening.   2. Garden ecology.   3. Biology.   I. Title.
[SB455.3.S9 1994]
635—dc20   94-16281   CIP

Contents

CONTENTS

Introduction to the 1994 Edition

I confess that I am still inordinately fond of ants—army ants, carpenter ants, fire ants, harvester ants, leafcutters, and weaver ants—the whole guild of species some 8,800 strong at last count, spread from the Arctic Circle to southernmost Tasmania. For a decade ants were my scholarly pursuit—from the brick sidewalks of Harvard to the mangrove swamps of Florida and the riverbank forests of Amazonia. A purloined flag bearing a strident blue ant on a field of red—a banner from the Costa Rican Communist Party—hangs above my three-volume set of Bailey's *Standard Cyclopedia of Horticulture*.

I am also, by now, quite accustomed to the surprise engendered by my myrmecological past. It isn't what people expect from someone working for a gardening magazine and television show. Mostly, I make light of the difference. After all, the tiniest manipulation of one's resume—the addition of the letters "pl"—are sufficient to turn an ant man into a horticultur-ist. But jesting aside, biology has served me well, and though I have shifted allegiance to another kingdom, I am very much the person of this book's subtitle. More than a decade after the original publication of *Earthly Pleasures*, I see that if I have come to garden at all well, it is in good measure because of my years among the social insects.

Specifically, I have been thinking about honeybees that a fellow graduate student, Tom Seeley, and I kept on the flat gravel roof of our laboratory at Harvard. These weren't re-search colonies, like the ants housed two floors below. We kept these hives for honey, the bees flying out over the rooftops of Cambridge, foraging on the locust and linden street trees and on the myriad other flowers found in the backyards and weedy margins of the city. In the fall we extracted fifty or more pounds of honey from each hive, left behind a good hundred pounds or so to keep the bees warm over the winter, and tried not to let too many bees into the building's elevator shaft.

You don't have to be a Ph.D. candidate to keep bees, but it definitely helps. The fact is, that unlike most of the organisms that we have exploited for thousands of years, the honeybee remains undomesticated. It is only within the last century that we have been able to deliberately breed honeybees at all, and most stocks remain the product of natural rather than artificial selection. In short, being a successful beekeeper means know-ing the ways of wild bees. Every advance in beekeeping— from the first smoke used by mesolithic hunters to calm colonies being raided for honey, to the first housing of colonies in sections of hollow tree trunk, to Reverend Lorenzo Lang-stroth's invention of the modern moveable-frame hive in 1851—has depended on taking advantage of the honeybee's biology. It is not surprising then that biologists should make good beekeepers and vice versa.

By contrast, gardeners are accustomed to working with domesticated organisms. The majority of our common food crops bear little resemblance to their antecedents. The seeds of corn and wheat, for example, no longer drop by themselves when ripe. Similarly, seed numbers have been dramatically increased, and their ripening concentrated into a short period that makes for an efficient harvest. Certain plant parts have become gigantic—the roots of carrots and parsnips, potato tubers, the leaves of cabbage, the fruits of apples and bananas. A shortening of the growing season and an increase of digestibility round out the changes.

But in the eight to ten thousand years that we have been gardening, many of us have been lulled into believing that we have completely tamed our charges. This is a conceit—one that is only being reinforced by genetic engineering. Plant domestication, as dramatic as it has been, has not stripped plants of their wildness entirely, and many of the plants we grow have yet to be significantly changed. The best gardeners, I have found, are those who remember their honeybees—who understand that even the most familiar organism still has its wild side. Being a biologist has proven to be a surprisingly useful way to understand wildflowers, or invasive weeds, or sauerkraut. In all of these things, there is still abundant natural history.

These essays, investigations of the science that lies behind the familiar, are in a sense applied biology. Rereading them, I am pleased to find them so sturdy. Yes, I know now why my experiments in woodchuck conditioning failed. Along with squirrels and chipmunks, woodchucks belong to that class of small mammals that spends much of its time in fright and flight. If panic left a mark on these creatures' psyches they would die of ulcers before reaching maturity. Terror is simply part of a woodchuck's world.

There is no amendment needed to the last chapter, though, which really was written on the eve of my wedding Elisabeth. Our optimism about the world remains; the only thing stronger is our optimism about each other. A framed copy of that essay hangs over our mantelpiece. We rarely consult it, for we know it now by heart.

—Roger B. Swain
June, 1994

Time, Energy, and Maple Syrup

You can't hurry maple syrup. The sap doesn't begin to flow from the sugar maples until there are nightly freezes and daily thaws, and even then the rate of flow depends more on how cold it got during the previous night than on how warm it becomes during the day. Even on the south side of the tree where the sap flows best, the drops form one at a time on the rounded lower tip of the metal spile and fall one at a time into the sap bucket hung beneath. It's not a sight for the impatient.

The boiling is no better. No matter how much wood you add or how much you fan the fire, once the sap is boiling, it is as hot as it's going to get. Even with a large, flat pan and a thick column of rising steam, the change from colorless sap to a light amber syrup is impressively slow. As a result, whether the syrup is being made out-

doors in pans recently liberated from the kitchen or in sug-
arhouses with evaporators whose English tin pans have
specially fluted bottoms to speed the boiling, one finds
oneself with a lot of time to think.

Once the fire has been built, the draft adjusted, and the
flow of sap tinkered with so that too much fresh sap from
the holding tank doesn't flow into the pan, then there isn't
much more to do except wait for the sap to become syrup.
You can't go away and work on anything else, because if
you do, the fire will die down and you'll lose the boil. You
can't just add a lot of wood at once either, because cold
wood will chill the fire and you'll lose the boil. So you end
up just watching the sap surge and roll in the pan, occasionally skimming off the dirty white foam that forms and
adding a stick of dry pine to the fire.

Some people think about next summer's garden while
the sap boils. They rotate crops in their heads, decide how
many rows of peas to plant, and remind themselves to pick
up some certified seed potatoes the next time they are in
town. Other people plan their investments, mentally rearranging and weeding their portfolios. A few boilers of sap
even contemplate the state of the union. I, on the other
hand, always end up thinking about maple syrup.

It's not the taste of the syrup that I think about. When
you're making it and sampling the hot liquor now and
then, you soon become tired of the flavor. My thoughts
are slightly grander. Wrapped in the steam rising from the
aluminum pan that rests on the concrete blocks of my
homemade evaporator, I continue on a mental odyssey. I
am searching for a reason to make maple syrup. Years ago
when I made it for the first time (a pint too dark to see

through), I was motivated by curiosity. But now I want an explanation for my continued interest in boiling sap, an explanation strong enough to explain why I spend eighteen hours at a stretch outdoors, my knees cooked, my beard singed, my feet freezing. The few gallons of sticky-sweet amber syrup scarcely seem adequate compensation for the long hours.

This search for justification is as time-consuming as the syrup making. Tentative justifications appear on the horizon, get mulled over, and are shared with friends who drop by to watch the sap boil. In recent years these have ranged from the metaphysical "It's magic" to the economic "It's cheap." Today it no longer seems like magic, and one visitor pointed out that even if I sold my entire year's production, I would still be earning only thirty-five cents an hour. I think his calculations were wrong, but I choose not to pursue a monetary justification anyway, just in case he is right. This year I've hit upon the idea that maple syrup is a fuel. It's a timely thought, brought on no doubt by the gas lines, nuclear power plant accidents, and legal suits over offshore oil drilling.

I don't want to give the impression that there is much else timely about my syruping operation. I still use some homemade wooden spiles made by whittling down sumac branches and boring out the soft pith. I also still use sap buckets, unlike modern syrup producers who use miles of plastic tubing and vacuum pumps that give them nearly twice as much sap from each taphole. In a sense I'm still at the stage of milking my trees by hand.

But the idea of maple syrup as a fuel intrigues me. What

I'm making with all this boiling is essentially a saturated sucrose solution containing 66.7 percent sugar. Assorted contaminants present in trace amounts give the syrup its flavor but add little to its fuel value. This value has already been calculated by nutritionists and dietitians—3,400 Calories per liter. (My one concession to timeliness is that my maple syrup musings have gone metric.) These Calories are actually kilocalories. That is, each Calorie is really one thousand small calories, each of which is defined as the amount of heat energy needed to raise one gram of water one degree Celsius. People who sell woodstoves never speak of calories. Instead they talk about British thermal units (Btu's), each of which is the amount of heat energy needed to raise one pound of water one degree Fahrenheit. Btu's and calories are readily interconverted. There are 251.9 calories in a Btu.

At this point I stop to skim off a spoonful of foam and flick it onto an adjacent snowbank.

To compute the Btu content of a liter of maple syrup, you simply divide three million four hundred thousand by 251.9. Long division like this done in one's head is slow, but there's time for these things. Allowing for what computer scientists call round-off error, I get 13,500 Btu's per liter. For comparison, a half kilogram of coal (1.1 pounds) contains 16,000 Btu's, and the same amount of gasoline, 23,000. In addition to tasting good (when you aren't making it), maple syrup thus contains a respectable amount of energy.

Since a liter of syrup is just about what you can get from a single taphole in one season, I began to perceive maple trees as gas pumps. That was easier than thinking of them as coal bins.

Because no one was around to share this discovery with, I went on to refine the argument, all the while keeping the fire stoked and watching the level of sap in the pan. I forced myself to consider the environmental impacts of maple syrup extraction. Critics of offshore oil wells on Georges Bank claim that they endanger a billion-dollar-a-year fishery, and opponents of strip mining are no more enthusiastic about plans to increase the burning of coal. My claim that "It's energy" would be just another short-lived justification if tapping the sugar maples threatened the forest, if it risked the loss of either the summer greenery or the autumn splendor.

Three hundred years ago it did. European immigrants learned to tap maple trees from the Indians. With a tomahawk or an axe, they cut deep gashes in the trunk, and below these they fixed a shingle to guide the flowing sap out away from the trunk so that it could fall into a vessel placed on the ground. After three or four years of such treatment, the average sugar maple tree expired. With a seemingly endless abundance of trees, the loss of a few could be dismissed, and this crude method of tapping persisted in some regions until 1860 or so.

Long before 1860, however, voices were raised in protest over such exploitation of the sugar maples. In 1790, *Remarks on the Manufacturing of Maple Syrup* by the Philadelphia Society of Gentlemen proclaimed that "although it has been found that the Sugar Maple tree will bear much hardship and abuse; yet the chopping of notches into it, from year to year, should be forborne; an auger hole answers the purpose of drawing off the sap, equally well, and is no injury to the tree." Whether because of an increased appreciation of maples or a declining supply of them, the protectionists ultimately prevailed. Today after two centuries of experimentation with the number, diameter, and depth of tapholes, it is safe to tap, year after year, even the most stately sugar maple in the middle of the front lawn.

To do this, the drill must be sharp, for a dull drill leaves a ragged hole that impedes the flow of sap and invites infection. A diameter of 1.1 centimeters (7/16 inch) is now standard. The hole should be drilled into sound wood a meter above the ground and at least 15 centimeters (6 inches) from any previous taphole that has not yet healed over. It is best to stagger the positions of the tapholes so that they aren't in the same vertical or horizontal plane. Angle the drill upward about ten degrees so that the hole will drain. Although 7.6 centimeters (3 inches) is a commonly recommended depth, 6.3 centimeters (2.5 inches) is better for the tree.

The number of tapholes in a given tree depends on its size. Trunks with a circumference of less than 79 centimeters (31 inches) shouldn't be tapped at all; from 79 to 112 centimeters (31 to 44 inches), one tap; from 113 to 152 centimeters (45 to 60 inches), two taps. Trees greater than 152 centimeters in circumference can have three tapholes drilled in them. If only one taphole is drilled, it should be on the south side of the tree, a second on the east, a third on the west.

Overtapping is dangerous, not because it removes too much sap from the tree, but because it promotes decay inside the trunk. When a tree is properly tapped, each tap-hole creates only a small zone of wounded and discolored wood, which is sealed off or compartmentalized by the tree. After a year or more the cambium grows to seal off the taphole. An excessive number of tapholes causes a co-alescing of discolored wood within the trunk. Decay in this wood spreads rapidly, and the trunk may be danger-ously weakened.

The growth of the cambium to seal off the entrance to the taphole will be delayed if the spile is driven into frozen wood or pounded in too firmly. This splits the cambium, causing a large area of cambium dieback beneath the bark, which takes a long time to heal over.

The most harmful practice in recent years has been the use, by some producers, of paraformaldehyde tablets in tapholes to increase and prolong the flow of sap. Recent research has shown that by inhibiting the natural sealing-off of the tree's vascular system, "the pill" promotes the growth of decay-causing fungi in the tree. This modern innovation is as detrimental to the health of the sugar ma-ples as the axe was three centuries ago.

To reduce the growth of bacteria and fungi in the tap-hole, which can reduce both the yield of sap and the health of the tree, it is permissible to squirt a dilute (1:10) solution of Clorox into the taphole after drilling, followed by a rinse with sterile water. Clean spiles are probably also helpful.

The trees I tap are mostly along the road, where it is easy to get to them when there's snow on the ground, and the syrup I make would become very expensive indeed if I had to include the cost of replacing any of them.

These thoughts kept me occupied most of the day, time enough to have converted the nearly tasteless sap into a panful of soon-to-be syrup. Blowing on a spoonful of it and sipping slowly, I could taste the energy. There's a satisfaction to being involved in something so justified. Then disaster struck. Just as I stooped to add more wood to the fire, I realized that I'd overlooked the energy being consumed in the boiling of the sap. Wood contains calories, too, and a lot of those were going up my stovepipe. I don't keep very good track of how much wood I use, and the wood I burn is an odd assortment of soft and hard wood with differing energy contents. But I remembered that commercial producers use about three liters of No. 2 fuel oil to make a liter of maple syrup.

Converting the liters of fuel oil into Btu's, I arrived at the staggering conclusion that it takes nearly nine Btu's of fuel to produce one Btu of maple syrup.

This was a terrible realization. To discover that I was using up more energy than I was gaining upset my Yankee sensibilities; it soured me on maple syrup. I considered quitting—I was that upset—and I might have, except that I stopped to take another taste of the magical elixir (I still believe a bit in its magical quality). The smooth, silken flavor of sap as it approaches syrup has a marvelous effect on the palate, and by connection, I suppose, on the mind. I recalled the energy statistics for the United States food system.

Year by year, the energy cost of each mouthful of our food has increased, until now we are using about ten times as much energy as our meals contain.

This is hard to believe, but it begins with agriculture itself. The tractors need gasoline, the irrigation pumps need electricity, synthetic fertilizers need natural gas. There are some crops like low-intensity potatoes that yield ten times as much energy as they use up, but others, like feedlot beef, use more than ten times as much energy as they produce. It all averages out to the figure that agriculture consumes about three times the amount of energy eventually consumed at the table. But the energy costs don't end with growing the food. Harvesting is followed by trucking and food processing. The manufacture of paper, glass jars, and metal cans used for packaging all require additional energy. The costs just keep adding up right through cooking the meal itself. The final tally is roughly ten calories spent for every calorie we swallow. The U.S. food system hasn't been at a break-even point since about 1910, and it seems destined to get worse.

There are voices of protest, just as there were two centuries ago in Philadelphia. The increased dollar cost of petroleum, the principal fuel of our food system, is forcing people to listen.

There are ways to reduce the costs of producing our food. These include using natural manures instead of synthetic chemical fertilizers and a system of integrated pest management instead of a strict reliance on synthetic pesticides. Plant breeders can devote more effort to selecting for resistance to pests, diseases, and drought. Using people to do the work on farms instead of machines means more hand labor, but it will be accompanied by a savings of energy.

Away from the farm there are savings to be made as well—shipping food by rail instead of in trucks and eating food that has not been elaborately processed. When I compare maple syrup production to the rest of the U.S. food system, it almost seems efficient. But of course it isn't, and there is just as much reason to worry about reducing its energy costs.

There are several things that can and are being done to make maple syruping more efficient. First, there is no reason to burn fuel oil. A few years ago when commercial producers were switching their wood-fired evaporators over to oil, about 70 percent of the Vermont producers decided not to. Now they're glad they stayed with wood. Petroleum should be saved as a resource for synthetic chemistry. Maple sap should be boiled with scrap wood, waste wood, and flammable refuse of other sorts. None of this will save energy overall, but it's a more intelligent use of resources. The savings of energy will come from new evaporators with improved designs, but that's a job for the technical inventor.

Second, anything that increases the sugar concentration of sap in the first place will save energy in boiling. While 2.5 percent is the average sugar content of sugar maple sap, trees have been found whose sap contains as much as 11 percent sugar. Such high-sugar maples might be propagated, although the thirty years needed for a tree to reach tappable size is a long time to wait. Commercial producers are experimenting with a process called reverse osmosis, whereby the sugar content of the sap is increased prior to boiling by forcing it through a semipermeable membrane, a sort of sieve through which only the water molecules can pass. The 11 percent sugar content of the sap that results requires much less energy to turn into syrup. However, the reverse osmosis process consumes energy too, and the overall savings are about 15 percent. A very old-fashioned technique, employed by the Indians, was to let the sap freeze in open pans and then discard the ice. The more concentrated sap that remained was then boiled, supposedly by dropping hot rocks into it.

Finally, it might be wiser to make thinner syrup. At present, maple syrup is boiled until it is a saturated solution. I am supposed to draw off my syrup when it reaches exactly 3.9 degrees Celsius (7 degrees Fahrenheit) above the boiling point of water. In fact, I'll draw it off while it's considerably thinner and finish it over a smaller fire. But even then I'm likely to can it a little thinner than the commercial producers are allowed to. They are bound by a series of strict regulations that specify that the syrup must be a specific density (66.5 degrees Brix or 36 degrees Baume) measured with a hydrometer. Roughly speaking, the sap must weigh eleven pounds per gallon.

My syrup weighs a lot less and hence takes less boiling, but I find it tastes every bit as good. My kidneys can remove the excess water a lot more efficiently than my homemade evaporator. I'm not suggesting thinner syrup as a way for commercial producers to begin selling less as more—I'm just offering it up as a way to save energy.

This is as far as I've come on my odyssey. Somewhere there is the ultimate justification for making maple syrup. The season for making it comes after the winter's energy crisis and before the spring's time crisis. It is late enough in the winter now not to have to worry about having enough fuel to get through, and early enough in the spring not to have to spend all one's time readying the garden. In this season the snow is soft and the sun seems warmer. Tending the fire and watching the sap boil may just be an excuse to be outdoors, and that may be the only justification. But until the buds swell and the sap turns cloudy, I intend to go on making maple syrup and taking the time to think of ways to save energy.

A Taste for Parsnips

Vegetable seed catalogs have replaced the penny candy store. The fireballs, the root-beer barrels, and the licorice whips aren't sold at the corner anymore. Now the sweets are sold by seed companies instead. There's 'Candystick' and 'Sweet Slice' and 'Sugar Rock,' but these aren't types of candy, they are varieties of sweet corn, cucumber, and muskmelon. Flipping through the pages of a seed catalog, one is reminded again and again of the confections that were once arrayed beneath a glass counter. 'Cherry Sweet' pepper, 'Honey Drip' muskmelon, 'Small Sugar' pumpkin, 'Sweetheart' carrot. The variety is as great as it was at the candy store, and it is no easier to make a selection now. How do you choose between 'Supersweet,' 'Sweet 'n Early,' and 'Earlisweet' muskmelons, or between 'Sugar Loaf,' 'Sugar King,' and 'Sugar Sweet' sweet corn? There is even 'Sweet Spanish' onion, 'Sugar

Hat' chicory, 'Sweet Meat' squash, and 'Sugar Lump' tomato. 'Short 'n Sweet,' 'Tiny Sweet,' 'Tendersweet' carrots. 'Sweet Mama' squash is followed by 'Sugar Baby' watermelon. There is no end to the sweet appellations. Yet one vegetable is missing from this sweet assemblage—the parsnip. None of the catalogs are calling the parsnip *sweet* anything. Leaf through some of them and you will find parsnips named 'All-America,' 'Avonresister,' 'Harris Model,' 'Hollow Crown,' 'Offenham,' and 'White Model,' but there are no names that mention sugar or sweetness. What makes this so surprising is that the parsnip is unequivocally sweet. The long, conical, white roots are far sweeter than any carrot, cucumber, or chicory, especially after they have been subject to freezing weather.

There is no proof that the parsnip was cultivated before the Middle Ages, but by the mid-sixteenth century, it was a staple vegetable in European gardens. In Thuringia, a state in central Germany, people evaporated the juice of parsnips to make a thick syrup that was eaten on bread instead of honey. Elsewhere parsnips were made into marmalade, a confection declared to excite the appetite and, at the same time, to be a proper food for convalescents.

The sugar in parsnips made them a logical choice for yeast fermentation, and the Irish made a beer from them by mashing the roots, boiling them with hops, and fermenting the liquor that resulted. The English preferred to make parsnip wine. An 1833 recipe by Mistress Margaret Dods says: "To every four pounds of parsnips, cleaned and quartered, put a gallon of water. Boil till they are quite soft, and strain the liquor off without crushing the parsnips. To every gallon of the liquor put three pounds of loaf-sugar, and a half-ounce of crude tartar. When nearly cold, put fresh yeast to it. Let it stand four days in a warm room, and then bung it up." Once bottled, parsnip wine should age before it's drunk. Some say two years is a minimum, others contend its quality improves for ten. Connoisseurs think it resembles the malmsey from the Madeira Islands. The bottle I was served contained a pale yellow wine, sweet and marvelously fortifying.

To fortify the stomach, plain parsnips are easier to prepare, but they mustn't be boiled, for that dissolves out the sugar. Steaming is better, but sautéing or baking are best. For an unusual and elegant dish, sprinkle parsnips with cinnamon, cover with mead, and bake at a low temperature until the mead has evaporated.

The sweetness of parsnips increases greatly after the roots have been exposed to freezing temperatures. Since parsnips are completely hardy and can remain in the ground all winter without being damaged, it is a common practice to wait until spring to harvest them. In 1694, Joseph Pitton de Tournefort wrote that in Lent, "they are the sweetest, by reason the juice has been concocted during the winter, and are desired at that season especially, both for their agreeable Taste and Wholesomeness. For they are not so good in any respect, till they have been first nipt with Cold." I dig mine in March as soon as the snow is off the ground, wading out through the soft, cold mud to claim the first harvest of the season.

This "concocting" of the juice to which Tournefort refers is a breakdown of starch into sugar. Because parsnips are sweeter when dug in the spring, it has always generally been believed that freezing was responsible for the change. But in 1922, Victor Boswell at the Maryland Agricultural Experiment Station investigated the changes in the sugar content of parsnips under different conditions of storage. He began his experiments on October 21. Some of the parsnips he dug and stored at 20 degrees Fahrenheit (minus 6.5 degrees Celsius), a temperature at which they were frozen solid. Others he dug and stored at 34 degrees Fahrenheit (1 degree Celsius). Still others he left in the field. For the next 149 days, until March 14, he periodically measured the amount of starch and sugar in the parsnips of each group.

In the field, the sugar content of the parsnips steadily increased. From an initial 16 percent sucrose on a dry weight basis, the parsnips sweetened to over 46 percent by March 14. On the other hand, the roots that were kept frozen during this time showed virtually no increase in the amount of sugar present. They contained a mere 18 percent sucrose by the end of the experiment. Thus freezing per se did not cause the starch to convert to sugar.

Boswell's startling finding was that the parsnips stored at thirty-four degrees Fahrenheit, just above freezing, became sweeter much faster than those left in the ground. At the end of a month's time they were already as sweet as the outdoor parsnips were after five months.

There are problems with long-term storage of parsnips in root cellars. They tend to dry out. Packing them in damp sand or earth will help prevent this. Boswell tried packing them in damp, yellow-pine sawdust, but they absorbed unpleasant flavors. If you want sweet parsnips for Thanksgiving, dig some in October and store them in the root cellar, but it is much easier to leave the rest outdoors until spring.

Regardless of whether the parsnips are harvested in the fall or in the spring, they are as large as they are going to get once freezing weather arrives. What size they are depends a great deal on how they are grown. For exhibition-size parsnips, conical holes three feet deep and six inches in diameter are dug, spaced twentyfour inches apart. These holes are filled with sifted compost, and only one parsnip seedling is allowed to grow in each. Such treatment results in the largest, most perfect parsnips but not the greatest yield per unit area. Growing parsnips too close together also results in a suboptimal yield, for individual plants compete with one another not only reducing the size of the parsnip but the weight of the total harvest as well.

Parsnips can be grown so as to produce an enormous amount in a very small area, more than three times the weight of carrots in the same space. Scientists at the National Vegetable Research Station at Wellesbourne in Warwickshire, England, report that for large rooted varieties such as 'Offenham,' the maximum yield is obtained if there are thirty-two plants per square meter (three per square foot). Theoretically, the parsnips will grow best if they are planted in a hexagonal grid, with each plant as far as possible from its nearest neighbor, thus minimizing competition. However, such spacing makes it terribly difficult to weed. Furthermore, additional experiments have shown that provided the ratio of between-row spacing to within-row spacing does not exceed 2.5 to 1, then the yield is not reduced. In practical terms, this means that for a parsnip density of thirty-two per square meter, the parsnips should be sown in rows, 27.5 centimeters apart (11 inches) and the seedlings thinned to 11 centimeters (4.5 inches) within the rows.

Parsnip seeds must be sown thickly, for they germinate slowly and unevenly. This is largely due to cold soil temperatures. Parsnip seeds germinate poorly below 45 degrees Fahrenheit (7 degrees Celsius), but the seeds must nevertheless be sown early in the spring to allow for the 120 days or so that the roots take to mature. (If the seeds are pregerminated at room temperature, 30 percent to 40 percent will have germinated within only seven days.) An additional cause of poor germination is poor viability of the seeds, since even under the best storage conditions, parsnip seeds last only three years. It is best to use new seeds each year.

Once the seedlings have germinated and have been thinned, the crop requires no attention other than an occasional weeding. Parsnips are an unusual root crop, for unlike carrots, beets, or turnips, the entire root is below ground. This protects the root from mice, which often eat the shoulders of carrots, but it makes them difficult to harvest in the spring when there are no tops to grab hold of. Plunging one's hands into icy muck to retrieve the roots is a springtime rite. All the roots should be harvested before they begin to develop new foliage, because parsnips are a biennial and all the food stored in the root will go into the production of a seedstalk.

In the light of the evidence that parsnips are delicious, nutritious, and prolific, one would expect them to be very popular. They aren't. Most seed catalogs offer only one variety, at most two or three, and most gardens have none at all. Ask someone why they aren't growing parsnips, and you are likely to provoke the following conversation:

> "I don't like parsnips."
> "What is it about parsnips that you don't like?"
> "The taste. I don't like the taste of parsnips."
> "Well, what is it about the taste that you don't like?"
> (Pause.) "I just don't like them, that's all."
> "Have you ever actually tasted parsnips?"
> "Well, no."

There's something about unfamiliar food that makes people think they won't like the taste. It's virtually impossible to convince a child to taste something new, and it's not much easier to persuade an adult. In both cases, the name that is given to the food is very important. Try giving tapioca the varietal name 'Fish-Eyes and Glue' and see if anyone will try it.

This brings us back to the proliferation of sweet names in seed catalogs. One almost suspects a conspiracy aimed at persuading children (and adults) to eat vegetables. Consider the edible podded pea for example. Names like 'Little Sweetie' and 'Sugar Snap' seem designed specifically to make this strange vegetable seem good to eat. Is 'Super Sweetpod' aimed at admirers of Superheroes? If 'Dwarf Gray Sugar' proves unappetizing, then there is always 'Mammoth Melting Sugar.'

I suspect that incorporating *sweet* or *sugar* into a name of a vegetable goes a long way toward assuring its popularity. Parsnips languish under such names as 'Offenham' and 'Hollow Crown.' Why not revive some of the sweet names for parsnips? I say revive, because seventy-five years ago seed catalogs contained a lot of them. In the *List of American Varieties of Vegetables for the Years 1901 and 1902,* a compendium of every name found in seed catalogs, the following names were used for 'Hollow Crown' parsnips: 'Improved Sugar,' 'Large Improved Sugar,' 'Large Sugar,' 'Long Sugar,' 'Long White Sugar,' 'Sugar Cup,' and simply 'Sugar.' Resurrect some of these names and parsnips may once again become a staple garden crop.

An old southern proverb says "Fine words butter no parsnips." They don't, but sweet ones will help people to take the first bite.

Of Cows
and Cowslips

Elsie: "What's that, Daddy?"
Father: "A cow."
Elsie: "Why?"
(*Punch*, 1906)

Distinguishing animals from plants is easy if you're a gardener: Plants remain rooted in one place, while animals come under, over, or through any fence intended to exclude them. The differences between plants and animals seem so obvious that we seldom give them a second thought—until someone asks us to elaborate.

For as long as anyone can remember, plants have been viewed as distinct from animals—plants' photosynthetic, rooted way of life in sharp contrast to animals' food-ingesting, mobile existence. Even the medieval pig boy, driving his herd through the forests of Europe, recognized that the oak trees, on whose acorns his charges fed, derived their nourishment in a manner different from animals, although he knew nothing of photosynthesis. Since then, much has been learned about chlorophyll and bacon production, but the boundaries between plants and animals, ironically, have become fuzzy.

The debate over what should be called a plant involves the so-called higher categories of classification. Taxonomists, those sainted professionals who have taken on the ostensibly boring task of naming new species and untangling the web of synonyms applied to old ones, also place organisms into larger groupings arranged according to the following scheme:

Kingdom
Phylum
Class
Order
Family
Genus
Species

Each succeeding category is a subgroup of the one above it, and all of the organisms in a category presumably have a common ancestor. The ultimate value of such a classification is that it gives a sense of the evolutionary relationships between organisms in the natural world. It also has resulted in recent controversy over just how many kingdoms actually exist.

Early taxonomists placed all living organisms into either the plant or the animal kingdom, a division reflected today in the twin disciplines of biology: botany and zoology. This simple dualistic classification of life worked fairly well until the microscope was invented and single-celled organisms were discovered.

A single drop of pond water can hold a vast menagerie of tiny, single-celled creatures, ranging from amoebas to paramecia. While some of them function as animals and some as plants, there are numerous creatures that fall somewhere in between. A famous example of this ambiguity is *Euglena,* a creature that is photosynthetic but also is able to swim rapidly, can be cultured in the dark, and whose nearest relatives have no chlorophyll at all. Both botanists and zoologists have studied *Euglena,* respectively claiming it to be a plant and an animal. The issue appears unresolvable. Many taxonomists prefer to call all single-celled organisms protozoa and to create a separate kingdom for them called Protista. It is an extremely diverse kingdom with multiple ancestors, though its diversity remains hidden from most of us by the microscopic nature of its inhabitants. Except for events such as red tide or amoebic dysentery—both caused by protozoa—most of us are unaware of these plant/animals.

Fungi, on the other hand, are extremely conspicuous, whether as fairy rings in a meadow, giant puffballs, or straw mushrooms in Chinese food. The mushroom's shape certainly suggests that it is a plant; however, the mushroom is not the entire organism. It is only the fruiting structure emerging into the air to disperse spores. The mushroom no more represents the entire fungus than the apple represents the entire apple tree. The bulk of the fungus consists of fine filaments, called hyphae, embedded in its food supply. Here the fungus, in a manner unlike plants or animals, feeds by absorption, sometimes secreting enzymes to break down material outside its body and absorbing the chemical compounds that result. This method of feeding, combined with the fact that there are no fungi that possess chlorophyll, is a strong argument for separating the fungi from the plants and classifying them as a separate kingdom: the Fungi.

Finally, in yet another category, there are the blue-green

algae, the photosynthetic organisms that produce dense algal blooms on the surface of water polluted by sewage or excess nutrients from agricultural runoff. Blue-green algae are not like kelp, Irish moss, or sea lettuce, all of which are plants, for these single-celled algae have no nucleus, no mitochondria (specialized internal energy centers), and no chloroplasts to contain the chlorophyll. In short, they have none of the internal structures characteristic of the cells of paramecia, poison ivy, puffballs, and people. This unusual cell structure is shared by only one other group, the bacteria, and together they have been given a special name. They are termed procaryotic cells, and it is widely believed that they are the ancestors of the eucaryotic cells that make up the rest of living organisms. It is also agreed that these procaryotic organisms need to be considered as a separate kingdom. This has been named the kingdom Monera.

If the procaryotic cell is the ancestor of the eucaryotic cell, how do you get from a sac containing undifferentiated raw materials to a cell with complex internal architecture? The most popular hypothesis is that the cells making up all of us are a symbiosis between procaryotic cells. Historically, a procaryotic cell somehow consumed another procaryotic cell that did not die, but instead multiplied and changed inside its host to become mitochondria. To create plant cells, the procaryotic ancestor also consumed blue-green algae that survived inside and became chloroplasts. Thus the cells making up a stalk of celery appear to be the result of an ancient partnership between several kinds of procaryotic cells. And because blue-green algae are most closely related to the individual chloroplasts within plant cells, it seems inaccurate to call them plants.

What is the outcome of this reclassification? Clearly, the two-kingdom system is outdated. There are too many organisms that are neither plants nor animals. At the very least, we should recognize Monera as a third kingdom. And it is perfectly reasonable to recognize Protista and Fungi as kingdoms four and five, although some taxonomists argue that the more kingdoms you have, the greater the confusion.

In any case, the next time you order a mushroom-growing kit from a seed catalog or the conversation turns to using single-celled algae as a food source, you will know you have entered a region of uncertain classification, somewhere between the chicken and the eggplant.

Seed Travels

South of Miami, about three low-pressure hours on a plane plus seven on an overcrowded bus and another in a slow dugout canoe, is a grove of pejibaye palms overlooking the Sarapiqui River on the Atlantic slope of Costa Rica. The attraction of this grove is not the palms themselves, although when boiled in salted water, the yellow, walnut-size fruits of *Bactris Gasipaes* are rich, mealy, and nutritious. Instead, the attraction is a small epiphytic vine, *Codonanthe crassifolia* of the family Gesneriaceae, growing in among the long needlelike spines that cover the palm trunks. *Codonanthe crassifolia* grows wild from southern Mexico to Peru, but most gardeners have seen it in hanging baskets: thick, elliptical, opposite leaves and a small, tubular, white waxy flower that is followed by a bright red berry. The plant is a welcome addition to any collection of gesneriads, but in suburban greenhouses or windowsills, there are seldom any ants.

Here in the pejibaye grove, where white-crowned parrots fly noisily overhead and the undergrowth is still dripping from the day's rain, the *Codonanthe* vines are firmly rooted in ant nests. Distributed on nearly a quarter of the palm trunks are dozens of flat, brown nests constructed of carton, a homogeneous material made up mostly of small bits of vegetable matter. While some of the nests are only a few centimeters across, others extend half a meter up and down the trunk, and all but the most recently constructed ones have *Codonanthe* vines growing out of them. Trails of ants lead from one nest to another, up and down the trunks and across the ground that separates the clumps of pejibaye palms. In fact, every nest in the grove is part of a single colony. The architects of this network of ant homes, this myrmecopolis, are shiny, black ants two to three millimeters long that bear the somewhat oversize name *Crematogaster longispina*. As tropical ants go, they are quite unremarkable, except for their taste in houseplants.

For Temperate Zone dwellers, who are accustomed to ants living beneath conical mounds of earth on sidewalks, the sight of arboreal ant nests may be surprising. But in the tropics, where there are no freezing temperatures to force ants to seek earthly warmth, many ants have taken to the trees. For the men who come to the grove every few weeks with their machetes to mow the lush vegetation that grows up between the trees, the ant nests on the trunks are of little interest. The men aren't especially interested in the *Codonanthe* vines either, for in this hot and humid atmosphere, they are accustomed to finding trunks laden with epiphytes of one kind or another.

To a foreign traveler, however, the sight of plants growing out of ant nests is unfamiliar and, depending on the traveler's proclivities, may inspire a closer look. The first recorded instance of a closer look involved a German named Ule who encountered *Codonanthe* vines growing out of ant nests in 1900, not in this grove but further south in the rain forests of Brazil. For Ule, as for subsequent investigators, the crux of the issue was: how did the plants get into the ant nest? From his observations he was to conclude that "the ants sow and care for these plants, which would otherwise be unable to exist, but in return enable the ants to construct arboreal nests insured against being washed away by the torrential rains and protected from the scorching rays of the sun." While he was at it, he coined the term "ant-gardens."

Twenty years later, Harvard's famous myrmecologist William Morton Wheeler encountered similar ant-gardens in Kartabo, Guyana. Without performing any further experiments, he found cause to criticize Ule's suggestion that the seeds were collected and sown by the ants. He counterproposed that the association was purely accidental. The ants were either constructing nests among the roots of established epiphytes, Wheeler claimed, or epiphyte seeds were accidentally falling onto established ant nests. While he was at it, he went on to say that Ule's hypotheses could be "regarded as a classical example of the uncritical mixtures of observation, inference, assertion and speculation, which abound in the work of observers in the tropics and constitute the only foundation on which some of the closet naturalists of Europe and the United States have been building their specious hypotheses."

There the matter stood until a young Radcliffe graduate,

Sally Kleinfeldt, arrived in the pejibaye grove overlooking the Sarapiqui River in September 1973. Her arrival was not that unusual, for in the last fifteen years this pejibaye grove has attracted more than its share of biologists, since it now belongs to the Organization for Tropical Studies, an international consortium of universities dedicated to getting naturalists out of the closets and into the tropics. Nine months after she stepped out of the dugout canoe, Kleinfeldt had discovered why the *Codonanthe* vines were growing out of the *Crematogaster* nests.

Like a great many plants, *Codonanthe crassifolia* possesses extrafloral nectaries, glands outside the flower that exude a sugary secretion collected by ants. There are from one to three of these nectaries at every leaf node, and from two to three ants are stationed at each node all the time. Probably to protect themselves from inclement weather while they feed, the ants construct shelters over the nodes of the vine. The ants don't intend to benefit the plants with these carton shelters, but the shelters are situated exactly where the plant produces adventitious roots. These roots grow into the carton, proliferate, and feed the vine from the nutrients present in the walls of the ant nest. It is as though the ants had provided the *Codonanthe* vine with potting soil. Almost certainly as a result of this feeding by ants, the vines growing on ant nests grow faster than those that occur on palm trunks without ants. Considering the care with which ants constructed the carton about the stems of the *Codonanthe* vine, Wheeler's assertion that the association was accidental appeared to be slipping, but it remained for Kleinfeldt to examine the fate of *Codonanthe* seeds to tip the scale firmly in favor of Ule.

At the base of developing fruits, there are five other ex-trafloral nectaries, and virtually all fruits are subtended by a cup of carton. Within this shelter, four to five ants tend the nectaries for the duration of the 35 to 55 days that it takes the berrylike fruit to mature. The ripe fruit then splits open along a single longitudinal line exposing 100 to 150 tiny pink seeds, each partially enclosed in a whitish aril. Although the red color of the fruit would suggest bird dispersal, shortly after the fruit splits, the ants enter and carry the seeds into their nests. There the fleshy aril is eaten, and the seed that remains is placed in the carton wall of the nest. The seeds could not have found a more suitable place for germination. A few weeks later, new seedlings are sticking out through the carton walls of the nest. Seeds that fall on the ground or bare bark will germinate as well, but the seedlings fail to grow. While the ants may not be consciously cultivating the plants in their gardens as Ule proposed, their faithful transport of *Codonanthe* seeds, fol-lowed by the placing of the seeds in an ideal site for growth, brings the ants and the vines into more of a mu-tally beneficial relationship than skeptical observers like Wheeler would have guessed.

The question of how *Codonanthe* seeds get into ant nests took nearly three-quarters of a century to resolve, a fact that reflects not so much the difficulty of the problem as the remoteness of the ant-gardens and the popularity of studying ants. People who lie on their stomachs watching ants carry off the remains of the picnic must be constantly ready to ward off cries of "Sloth," and many a profes-sional ant researcher has vowed to study flamingos next time, since no one will ever ask, "How do I get rid of flamingos?"

Studying ants can be entertaining, however. And for those who have a low threshold of discomfort (who don't like overcrowded buses), there is no need to go off to the tropics. There are several plants in the woods of North America whose seeds are carried about by ants.

In Worcester, Massachusetts, on July 14, 1939, Burton Gates went to his garden to collect fresh seeds of *Trillium grandiflorum,* the white wake-robin. Although a number of seed capsules had fallen to the ground, they were all empty. The next day there were more empty capsules, but tipped off by the presence of an ant in one of them, Gates offered her (all ant workers are female) a freshly harvested seed. She grasped the seed in her mandibles, and, followed by Gates, she proceeded to her nest beneath a stone pile five meters (fifteen feet) away. There discarded among the rocks, Gates found his missing *Trillium* seeds.

A partial list of species whose seeds are regularly dispersed by ants includes *Asarum canadense, Hepatica acutiloba, Nemophila Menziesii, Sanguinaria canadensis, Stylophorum diphyllum, Trillium grandiflorum, Uvularia grandiflora,* and several *Viola* species. Many more ant-dispersed species have been discovered in Europe than in North America—more than one hundred species in forty genera—but this probably says as much about the number of ant watchers as it does about the number of ants.

Myrmecochory, as seed dispersal by ants is technically called, depends on the seeds being attractive to ants. Most ant-dispersed seeds have an elaiosome, or oil body, an appendage that is so termed because it often contains drops of an oily substance. The elaiosome prompts the ant to seize the seed and carry it back to her nest, mistaking the seed for a tasty bit of dead insect or, possibly in some cases, one of her own larval sisters. Inside the nest other ants strip off the elaiosome, and, finding the seed is either inedible or fake, they discard it in a general refuse pile. The *Crematogaster* in the pejibaye grove deposited their *Codonanthe* seeds in the carton walls of their nest, but in the Temperate Zone the ants usually dump the seeds outdoors.

Because worker ants can't fly, they can't transport the seeds very far away from the parent plant. Critics claim that a dispersal distance of a few yards is too little to be of any real significance. For a *Codonanthe crassifolia* seed, being left in a nutrient-rich, moist, carton wall of the nest is clearly beneficial, but what about other plants whose seeds are simply discarded outdoors? Is there any benefit to the plant?

Apparently there is, for several plants with ant-dispersed seeds have evolved structures in addition to elaiosomes that make it easier for the ants to get at their seeds. The sedge *Carex pedunculata,* for example, has decumbent culms that proffer the plant's seed to ants at ground level. While studying the population biology of woodland sedges in the Six Mile Creek ravine in Ithaca, New York, Steve Handel from Cornell University discovered that *Carex pedunculata* was ant dispersed and further was able to show exactly how the sedge benefits from having ants carry off its seeds.

This low-growing sedge has dark green leaves that persist during the winter. In April a new rosette of leaves begins to develop along with fertile culms that elongate, bend down, and release their mature seeds in May. Each seed has a broad, white elaiosome at its base, which causes ants to carry off the seed. Two other species of sedge, *C. plantaginea* and *C. platyphylla,* also occur in the same woods, but neither is ant dispersed. When he offered seeds of *C. pedunculata* and *C. plantaginea* to a laboratory colony of ants, he found that all of the *C. pedunculata* seeds were carried into the nest, the elaiosomes removed, and the seeds discarded, while none of the seeds of the other species were touched. Handel then experimented with growing various combinations of the sedge species in pots. Most interestingly he found that *C. pedunculata* is a poor competitor. When grown in company with the other sedge species, the *C. pedunculata* produced fewer rosettes, fewer flowering culms, and less dry matter.

Accompanying this finding was Handel's observation that although all three sedge species grew in the same woods, they were not growing in exactly the same places. The *C. pedunculata* were growing on rotten logs. Twenty-eight percent of the rotten logs had *C. pedunculata* on them.

Compared to most forest processes, a rotten log has a very short life. It is an excellent microhabitat for plant growth, but most plants have no way of colonizing it before the log disappears. How does *C. pedunculata* get its seeds onto a rotten log? The ants carry them there. The ants are nesting in the log themselves, and their refuse piles are on the log's surface. Discarded *C. pedunculata* seeds are free to germinate and grow without competition, for the other sedge species can disperse their seeds only a culm's length from the parent plant. On the short-lived but un-populated rotten logs, *C. pedunculata,* the poor competi-tor, can flourish without interference from other sedge species.

Findings like these suggest that other plants may be benefiting in the same way from having their seeds carried off by ants. While the ants cannot carry the seeds a great distance, the end point of the seed's travel may be very important for the seedling's subsequent survival. In many cases the ants may assure the seedling both fertile ground and freedom from competition. New cases of seed dispersal by ants are certain to be found, and similar studies should help to explain the seemingly erratic occurrence of wildflowers. Some day we'll know how many more plants owe their distribution to travels with an ant.

Tree Bark

Tree bark, like French, becomes much more relevant when you have an immediate need to understand it. If, for example, you decide rather late in the winter that you are going to be self-sufficient in the pancake department and make your own maple syrup, you may find yourself out in the woods with a bit and brace, a bag of metal spouts, and a growing realization that you aren't quite sure which trees are sugar maples. This invariably leads to an intensive study of tree bark, because there is nothing more embarrassing than having someone else point out that you have tapped an elm.

Fortunately, a great many tree species can be identified by their bark. Looking around, it is easy to recognize the sycamores, whose trunks are mottled with pale green and white patches where large flakes of gray bark have fallen off. The shagbark hickories also stand out because of the rough, hard, curved strips of bark that warp away from the trunks. Because of the limited range of colors in tree barks, texture is often the most useful character in distinguishing species. Even with your eyes closed, it is easy to tell the yellow birch (small, tight curls of bark) from the paper birch (large sheets of chalky, peeling bark) or the gray birch (smooth bark that rarely peels at all). The sugar maples you seek have deep, vertical furrows in the hard bark, while the swamp maples, which yield a poor quality of sap, have flaking bark with shallow furrows.

If you remove a strip of bark from a trunk, you will expose the vascular cambium that surrounds the wood, a layer that is responsible for the annual increase in the trunk's diameter. The strip of bark you hold consists of two zones—the inner and the outer bark.

The inner bark contains the phloem: cells that are produced by divisions of the vascular cambium and, in turn, are responsible for transporting the products of photosynthesis from the leaves to the roots. Girdling a tree trunk by removing a strip of bark all the way around will kill the tree because it interrupts the food flow and starves the roots. Even when left undisturbed, the phloem cells do not last forever, for as the trunk increases in girth, they are crushed and ruptured. New phloem cells, replacements for the old, are produced by the vascular cambium, that vital mantle wrapped about the trunk.

The outer bark, which is usually inseparable from the inner bark, consists of a second cambium—the cork cambium—and the cork tissue it produces. This cork forms an exterior wall of dead cells that are made waterproof and airtight by a chemical called suberin. In birches the cork cambium produces two types of cork cells in alternating layers; as a result, birch bark freely separates into thin sheets of cork.

The cork of tree bark is so airtight that the underlying tissues would suffocate if there were not breathing pores, called lenticels. In bottle corks, which are made from the cork of the European cork oak *(Quercus suber)*, the lenticels are conspicuous as dark brown channels running from one side of the cork to the other. If the lenticels ran the length of the cork, it would not be airtight and champagne would lose its fizz.

The different textures in tree bark result from changes in the cork cambium and the stretching of the bark as the tree increases in circumference. In the beech tree the cambium remains close to the surface, expanding when necessary and producing a smooth gray cork that appears tightly stretched over the trunk. In most species, however, successive cork cambiums are formed beneath the original one: the new layer of cork that forms cuts off and kills the outer cambium, which eventually rips apart under pressure from the expanding trunk. Some trees, such as pines and sycamores, have secondary cork cambiums that occur in patches. With time these patches result in layers of scales, easily seen in a fragment of pine bark. Like pines, ash trees have patches of secondary cork cambium, but these form within phloem tissue containing long fibers. As the trunk expands, the fibers pull apart, creating a net of diamond-shaped furrows, but the bark does not flake off in scales.

Whether you are out in the woods to tap trees or to cut logs, the differences in tree bark soon make you take off your gloves just to feel the trunks, for no sculpture garden ever offered such a range of textures or was so tolerant of handling. Slapping or prodding tree bark does it no harm, for the function of the bark is to protect the tissues underneath. In the winter it guards against dehydration, sharp changes in temperature, and the gnawing of hungry mice, rabbits, and deer who are in search of winter browse. In the warmer months it also serves as a barrier to invasion by fungi and boring insects and as an insulating layer that may help the tree to survive small brushfires burning around its base.

To properly protect the tree, the bark must remain in a continuous layer: gaps will permit infection to enter. Cutting into the bark causes wound cork to form quickly; many of the holes you drill into sugar maples, for example, will seal over in a year. In the smooth-barked beech, wound cork is visible for a century or more, and the inscribing of names is an age-old custom. The penknife that carved RS + EW into the smooth bole was only tracing a tradition described by Shakespeare when he wrote:

> O Rosalind! these trees shall be my books,
> And in their barks my thoughts I'll character.

Most trees, however, have no writing on them. The tree bark is its own language, and learning the vocabulary—ash bark, beech bark, cherry bark, oak bark—is something you do after you have cut a cord of poplar for the fireplace or hung a sap bucket on an elm. The learning may be motivated by necessity, but like a foreign language, having the skill is a long-term pleasure. Bare trees are no longer just gray trunks in the forest; they become invested with a brocade of individuality.

Skototropism:
A Shady Behavior

Houseplants are like the yeast cultures once used to make sourdough bread. The plants have been household occupants for so long that we can no longer remember when they first appeared or where they came from; we culture them by placing a small propagule, like a spoonful of yeast-starter, into a pot full of fresh nutrient medium; and when we travel from residence to residence the houseplants are carried with us. In the process of domestication, however, houseplants have lost much of their vitality, complexity, and interest, qualities that come from an organism's interaction with its natural environment. Small wonder then that so many houseplants are left to languish on windowsills, photosynthesizing feebly, their aliveness the only quality that prevents them from being discarded.

A visit to the native habitat of a familiar houseplant, or a review of the botanical literature, can do much to revive interest in a specimen's existence. *Monstera deliciosa* has a dozen common names, including split-leaf philodendron, Swiss-cheese plant, and ceriman. Certainly one of the most common houseplants, it is a native of the wet tropical forests from Mexico to Panama. In northern homes the dusty foliage draped over a slab of rough-barked wood seems unrelated to the robust vines clambering over the tropical tree trunks. In the forest the foliage is a dark, shiny green; deep slits in the leaves end with a series of holes or "fenestrations" in the middle of the blade; and the plant blooms freely in sunlight, the flower consisting of a spadix and spathe characteristic of other plants in the family Araceae such as jack-in-the-pulpits, anthuriums, and skunk cabbages. Fourteen months after the cream-colored flowers appear, the twenty- to twenty-five-centimeter- (eight- to-ten-inch-) long fruit ripens, cucumber shaped, its skin marked with a hexagonal pineapple-like pattern. As it ripens, the skin splits away from the grayish-white flesh within. Eating the immature fruit can be painful because there are sharp calcium oxalate crystals in it which will irritate the tender skin of your mouth; when the fruit is slightly overripe, however, it is delicious. Some authorities think it tastes of pineapple, others of pineapple and banana. Richard Schultes, plant explorer and director of Harvard's Botanical Museum, says that the fruit of *Monstera deliciosa* tastes like a mixture of pineapple and strawberries.

The first recorded encounter between Europeans and *Monstera deliciosa* occurred in 1832 when Wilhelm Frederick Karwinsky von Karwin collected specimens in Mexico. Sent to Munich, the specimens elicited no response.

However, when Frederick Liebmann sent some from Mexico to Copenhagen in 1842, and Joseph Warszewicz sent others from Guatemala to Berlin in 1846, the plant was declared a horticultural triumph. Mike Madison, of the Selby Arboretum in Florida, who has recently revised the taxonomic classification of the genus *Monstera,* believes that most of the specimens cultivated today are direct descendants of those collected by Liebmann and Warszewicz over a hundred years ago.

Nineteenth-century plant hunters were looking for new plants to introduce into their own countries. Sturtevant in his *Notes on Edible Plants* mentions that *Monstera deliciosa* was cultivated under glass in England specifically for its edible fruit. Today, books listing specialty fruits for southern Florida recommend ceriman fruit for dessert or fruit punches.

Now, less interested in enhancing botanical or horticultural collections, scientists working in tropical forests are seeking more information about the biology of *Monstera.* Fundamental questions about its pollination and seed dispersal remain to be answered. At present it is known that the temperature of the *Monstera deliciosa* flower increases fifteen degrees Celsius (twenty-seven degrees Fahrenheit) above the air temperature when the pollen is ripe. Is this a mechanism to attract heat-seeking pollinators? It has been suggested that the slits and holes in the large leaves serve to break up the layer of still air surrounding the leaf surface and thus prevent it from overheating in full sun.

Most recently two researchers, Donald Strong, a professor at Florida State University, and Tom Ray, a graduate student at Harvard, have been studying a relative of *Mon-*

stera deliciosa named *M. tenuis*. This species of *Monstera* is a vine that passes through three distinct morphological stages during its life. When the seed, having fallen to the forest floor, germinates, it sends out a thin green stem only one millimeter in diameter and leafless except for tiny bractlike leaves at the nodes. When this thin vine encounters a tree trunk a few meters away from its point of germination, it enters the second stage and begins to put out flat saucer-shaped leaves that press close to the trunk in an overlapping pattern as the vine grows up the tree. Two types of adventitious roots develop out of the climbing stem. One type is short and has disks on the root hairs that serve to anchor the vine to the trunk. The second type is several meters long and grows earthward where it then proliferates and provides nutriment to the arboreal plant, which may no longer have any stem connection to the ground. As the shingle-plant form of the vine grows upward, the saucer-shaped leaves become bigger and bigger, but they do not exceed fifteen centimeters (six inches) in diameter. When the tip of the vine reaches the sunlight striking the tree trunk in the upper reaches of the forest, it begins to put out leaves as long as two meters (six feet), with deep slits extending almost to the midrib. The leaves are no longer pressed close to the trunk, but instead they hang out away from the trunk. It is at this third stage that the plant flowers and fruits.

The discovery of Strong and Ray is that the first stage vine, the thin green fiber creeping along the forest floor, is actually growing toward the darkest portion of its horizon. The dark silhouette toward which it heads, at a top speed of ten centimeters (four inches) per month, is usually a large tree up which it will be able to climb into the sunlight. Strong and Ray have shown that the seedlings are not simply growing away from the light. Given a choice between a light source and a dark source arranged ninety degrees from one another in an artificial situation, the *Monstera tenuis* seedlings grew toward the dark source instead of directly away from the light source as they would have if the vines were negatively phototropic. In the forest when seeds have fallen about the base of a tropical tree, the seedlings all grow toward it creating a wheel with short green spokes and the tree trunk as hub. Once the vines reach the tree trunk or any tall vertical surface they become phototropic and grow toward the light. The two researchers have found that if the vine is allowed to grow into a low box laid on its side it will become phototropic when it reaches the darkest part of the box and begin to grow toward the entrance again. But when it reaches a lighter region of the box it reverses and grows toward the dark again. Switching back and forth, the seedling will oscillate just inside the box until its energy is exhausted. This does not ordinarily occur in nature, as the shoot tip is held erect while the vine grows, enabling it to avoid minor cul-de-sacs on the forest floor.

Seeking a new word for their discovery, Strong and Ray asked Mary Thornton, a classicist, to coin a Greek word for "growth toward a silhouette." She replied: "It is impossible to find a Greek word for silhouette exactly, because this word is named after a Frenchman named Etienne de Silhouette, 1767, who was a Controller-general of finances." They finally settled on *skotos,* the Greek word for darkness or gloom, and coined the word skototropism to describe an organism's movement toward it.

Virtually all plants depend on direct solar radiation for

their energy, and it is unusual for them to grow toward the dark. The discovery of skototropism suggests that tropical vines have a complex behavioral repertoire. To the scientist this is an invitation for investigation. For the gardener it should invest an old familiar houseplant with an exotic aura. Although the *Monstera deliciosa* at the end of the couch may never be robust enough to yield fruit, it should still be able to feed its owner's imagination.

Salting the Earth

Salt ruined the sledding again this winter. The big yellow Public Works truck, orange warning lights flashing, flung salt all up and down the street before the snow had a chance to build up. Children, who had expectantly waxed the runners of their sleds for greater speed, helplessly flung back snowballs and angry words before dragging their Flexible Flyers back into the house.

At the time, adults were grateful for the road salt. As the granules of sodium chloride mixed with water on the street, they dissolved to make a brine that froze only at temperatures well below thirty-two degrees Fahrenheit (zero degrees Celsius). Sodium chloride was the salt most commonly spread by the trucks, and it kept the asphalt ice-free down to ten degrees Fahrenheit (minus twelve degrees Celsius). At colder temperatures, the road crews mixed in some of the much more expensive calcium chloride, since that type of salt prevented the road from freezing even at minus forty degrees Fahrenheit (minus forty degrees Celsius). The bare pavement that resulted from the use of de-icing salt was certainly easier to drive on; conditions weren't much different from those in midsummer.

Now, months later, with crocuses blooming beside basement windows, the snow and the ice are no longer a problem, but the road salt is. We all have white, highwater marks staining the leather of our shoes, and the evergreens between the house and the road look as though they have been visited by a flock of pigeons. Elsewhere the salt is corroding automobile bodies, damaging concrete, and jeopardizing the health of people who have high blood pressure by contaminating drinking water supplies with sodium. Of considerable interest to gardeners, however, is the effect the salt has on plants.

Even the most unobservant pedestrian can see that many of the roadside trees are not healthy. The saplings that have been planted recently don't seem to be growing very fast. A few of them, still fastened to their support stakes, are dead. Some of the older trees, especially the sugar maples, bristle with dead twigs, and their leaves turn color prematurely in the fall.

For years salt has been an obvious suspect. Back in the 1950s, just as the highway department's "bare pavement" policy was becoming generally accepted, researchers set out to discover if road salt could injure trees; it soon became apparent that in sufficient amounts, salt was fatal. In one experiment conducted by the Shade Tree Laboratories of the University of Massachusetts, ten pounds of sodium chloride was spread over the root system of a sugar maple in the winter of 1954, and the treatment was repeated weekly throughout the year. By spring, all the grasses and herbaceous plants under the tree were dead, and after four years the tree itself died: the salt concentration of the soil it was growing in increased from less than ten parts per million to eight hundred ppm.

The sugar maple was not the only species that proved to be salt sensitive. Red maple, shagbark hickory, American elm, and basswood, as well as red pine, white pine, and hemlock were injured by the spreading of salt. Some other tree species, however, proved to be tolerant of road salt: red and white oaks, black, yellow, gray, and paper birch. Black locust, white ash, black cherry, and red cedar also withstood extra salt.

Calcium chloride was once spread on dirt roads during the summer, since it absorbed water from the air, dampened the road surface, and kept down the dust. Thus the year-round application of salt used in the experiments was not atypical. But with the passing of the dirt road, summer salt use has declined. Some experiments that use only winter applications of salt show little or no injury to the trees. While everyone agrees that enough salt can be fatal, the issue is now one of determining the effect of sublethal doses. The research is still incomplete.

It is difficult to obtain conclusive findings, because the roadside of a new suburban development is a complex environment. For instance, soil type, water level, drainage patterns, rainfall, and individual genetic variation from tree to tree determine what effect road salt will have. Even without salt, the trees are subject to a barrage of ill-treatment, including soil compaction, inadequate watering, air pollution, collisions with automobiles, gas leaks, lawn herbicides, and excessive pruning to clear power lines. It is a wonder that any survive.

But the multitude of hazards does not absolve road salt. The stresses of roadside life can act synergistically on a tree: when two harmful conditions occur simultaneously, the injury to the tree is greater than the sum of the effects either condition would produce alone. Even moderate levels of salt in the soil or on the foliage may very well act in concert with other pressures to bring about tree injury.

There is no reason to think that we can indefinitely load additional salt into the roadside environment without changing the vegetation. In the long run, salt-sensitive species growing alongside heavily salted roads will probably be replaced naturally by salt-tolerant ones. Naturalists should monitor the species composition of roadsides, not limiting themselves to the immediate vicinity, because high-speed vehicles will whip up a plume of salt spray that can drift sideways, damaging foliage hundreds of feet from the road. Only by continuing to study the effects of road salt can the true costs of ice-free roads be measured.

The discovery that salt is harmful to plants is not novel. Cultures that rely on irrigation water for agriculture have been cursed for thousands of years by excess salt accumulating in their soils. The purest spring water contains some dissolved salt, and when water evaporates after being spread on cultivated fields, it leaves salt behind. If there is not enough rainfall to wash the salt away, extra irrigation water must be used to flush the soil. But in an arid region where people, livestock, and crops must compete for limited water, there is often not enough to "waste" on flushing the fields. As years pass, the soil becomes saltier and saltier until there is a white crust of crystals on the surface: crops can no longer be grown, and agricultural man must move on or succumb. The destructive power of salt was known to ancient armies that once used salt as a form of chemical warfare. " [They] beat down the city and sowed it with salt" reads the Old Testament. Today a quarter of the irrigated land in the United States yields less than it should because of excess salt.

The first indications that salt is accumulating in the soil are blue green leaves, stunted plants, and a smaller harvest. At higher concentrations, the tips or margins of the leaves may die—the dead sections sharply separated from the healthy part of the leaf. In such saline soil, seeds may not germinate. If gardeners suspect salt in their soil, they can send a soil sample to the nearest agricultural experiment station. There an electrical conductivity test will be performed to determine the amount of dissolved salts in a soil extract. A second, more elaborate, and less available test involves actually measuring the sodium and chlorine content of the plants themselves.

Just as oaks and hemlocks differ in their sensitivity to salt, so do the various fruits and vegetables. The presence of 1,500 ppm of salt in the soil affects the growth of radishes, beans, and strawberries. Avocados, citrus, peach, pear, or plum trees may yield less fruit. At 3,000 ppm most garden vegetables grow poorly; above 5,000 ppm only a few salt-tolerant crops such as asparagus, kale, beets, date palms, and cotton grow satisfactorily. A salt concentration of 5,000 ppm is equivalent to 0.5 percent of

the soil. Since seawater contains 3.5 percent salt, it is understandably toxic to vegetation when it is driven inland
by hurricanes or tidal waves.

At first the stunted growth of crops in saline soil was
attributed solely to "physiological drought." As the salt
concentration in the soil surrounding the roots increases,
so does the osmotic pressure, and the plants, so the theory
goes, are unable to absorb enough water for normal
growth. But recently it has been discovered that most
plants can adjust to increased salt levels and continue to
absorb water. However, when the sodium and chloride
ions themselves are absorbed, they interfere with photosynthesis and other metabolic processes, thus stunting the
plant. Excess sodium ions in the soil may also affect the
plant's nutrition by reducing the availability of other ions.
At higher concentrations, the sodium ions displace the calcium ions, and the soil becomes hard and compact. But by
tilling gypsum (calcium sulfate) into soils that have been
flooded with seawater by hurricanes, it is possible to re-
store tilth to the soil.

Of course, there are large sections of the world that have
naturally salty soils. Plants growing in salt marshes, mangrove swamps, and salt deserts have evolved to live with
high levels of salt. Asparagus, a garden vegetable that is so
salt tolerant that in colonial times salt was spread in the
row to keep the crop weed-free, is a native of the Mediterranean shore. Halophytes (from the Greek word *halas* for
salt) have evolved a number of ways to handle the salt.
Some, like the rush *Juncus gerardi,* simply accumulate salt
in their tissues and dump it yearly when they discard their
leaves. Others take in more water to dilute the salt. This

leads to a high degree of succulence as in the marsh sam-phire, *Salicornia stricta*. Finally, a third group possesses salt glands to secrete excess salt. Salt-tolerant plants like Japanese black pine or the wild *Rosa rugosa* are of special interest to seaside gardeners, for they can withstand salt spray and an occasional flooding with seawater.

Most of the plants we grow, however, are adapted to low-salt soils. For centuries gardeners in arid lands have worried about salt buildup. In the snow belt, concern over road salt is relatively recent but is equally justified. Salt may be a wonderful addition to corn on the cob or cucumber salad, but salt in the garden is no great shakes.

The Education
of a Woodchuck

Still wearing my pajamas, I sneak across the lawn toward the herb border. The woodchuck senses something and stops chewing a sprig of parsley only halfway eaten. I freeze. The cold, wet grass under my bare feet threatens to make this a reality, but I am intent on remaining motionless. Then he blinks and resumes eating my precious parsley. I take two more stealthy steps. This time he halts for a second only and then gallops for the woods. With a roar I am after him, charging through the blueberries and meadowsweet, nearly catching up just as he disappears down a burrow dug beneath a juniper bush. Well warmed by the chase, I go indoors to have breakfast, pleased to have gotten so close.

In these bloodcurdling charges, I am not trying to catch the woodchuck, I am trying to educate him. I figure that if I can get close enough to scare him, then he will become conditioned to avoid my garden and will feed elsewhere. If panic and parsley become intimately associated in his mind, he may learn to prefer clover. This technique is the current culmination of my woodchuck studies. I have never had to explain my behavior to my neighbors, who fortunately live out of sight. Many of them have defended their gardens against woodchucks for generations, and they automatically resort to more sanguinary methods of control. They purchase smoke bombs from the hardware store that give off a poison gas when lit and placed down the entrance to the burrow. Some set traps, others keep a gun handy. One elderly gentleman I know spends late afternoons sitting beside his vegetable garden with a half can of Rolling Rock beer and a bowl of homemade pickled herring. When a woodchuck appears, he takes a shot at it. If he misses, he follows it to its hole and dynamites the burrow. Woodchuck control tends to invite individuality.

People who shoot woodchucks because their grandfathers shot woodchucks are very likely to have inherited an anthropocentric view of life. Their beliefs are descendant from the dominion-over-the-earth concept of Genesis. Organisms tend to be judged thumbs up or thumbs down, depending on whether they contribute to or detract from man's immediate needs; and their behavior is described in human terms. This approach to woodchucks was nicely summed up in a report presented in 1883 to the New Hampshire legislature recommending a bounty be established for woodchucks. In part the report read:

> The Woodchuck, despite its deformities of both mind and body, possesses some of the amenities of a higher

civilization. It cleans its face after the manner of squirrels, and licks its fur after the manner of a cat. Your committee is too wise, however, to be deceived by this purely superficial observance of better habits. Contemporaneous with the ark, the Woodchuck has not made any material progress in social sciences, and it is now too late to reform the wayward sinner. . . . The Woodchuck is not only a nuisance, but also a bore.

When the woodchuck committee filed its report, the science of ecology did not exist. From woodchucks to wolves, pests were to be eliminated whenever possible. Today, however, the wolves are known to be responsible for regulating the populations of deer and moose, keeping these animals from becoming so numerous that they destroy their own food supply and ultimately themselves. There is now a growing realization that beavers, fishers, and hawks all provide essential services—an awareness that the living community has evolved both to accommodate and to rely on their existence. "Everything is connected to something" is a popular phrase; eliminate any species and you are most likely to create discord.

As a scientist, I thought this applied to all animals including woodchucks. But when I went out to my garden on one April morning and found an entire row of green stubs where yesterday there had been a promising row of Chinese peas, my convictions were sorely tried. Couldn't I make an exception to my rule that every species has a place and shoot the woodchuck? In 1844, Karl Marx said no, that "one basis for life and another for science is a priori a lie." But they don't have woodchucks in Europe, and I don't know that Marx had a vegetable garden. The simplest solution to the dilemma seemed to be to discover that the woodchuck had no real value (other than as stew). Therefore, I set out in search of a scientific justification for shooting one.

The woodchuck, I learned, is the largest member of the squirrel family, reaching twenty-seven inches in length and weighing up to fourteen pounds. It attacks gardens from Maine to Georgia and as far west as Nebraska. Its Latin name, *Marmota monax,* comes from the Latin word for marmot and an Indian word meaning "the digger." *Woodchuck* is apparently an alteration of the Cree Indian *wuchak,* meaning fisher, marten, or weasel. Other common names include groundhog and whistle-pig.

The woodchuck emerges from its winter burrow in early spring, before the snow is gone but seldom as early as February 2, Groundhog Day. While the females remain close to their burrows, the males move about, especially on moonlit nights, looking for mates. The period of cohabitation is brief: gestation takes only thirty days and as delivery approaches, the female drives the male away. From two to nine young are born, each only four inches long, naked, blind, and one ounce apiece. After a month they weigh half a pound and are ready to leave the burrow, at which point they are preyed upon by foxes, coyotes, bobcats, weasels, minks, owls, and large snakes. The timber rattler reportedly even enters burrows in search of young woodchucks. Shortly after they leave the burrow, the young are weaned. They disperse to establish their own burrows and to assume the essentially solitary life of an adult woodchuck.

In early summer, woodchucks feed both in the early morning and late afternoon. Later in the season, they are most active from an hour before sunset until dark. Their diet is 99 percent vegetarian. When snow covers the ground, they may feed on bark and twigs of trees and shrubs. Later in the year, they eat large quantities of legumes such as clover and alfalfa. If vegetable gardens are available, they will eat peas, beans, corn, strawberries, raspberries, cherries, cantaloupes, cabbage, kale, and beet greens. On rare occasions, they will eat a grasshopper or June bug.

In spite of its short legs and wobbling gait, the woodchuck can climb twenty feet up a tree, and W. T. Cox in 1926 found a woodchuck swimming across the Mississippi River.

By fall the woodchuck has put on a great amount of fat. He moves from his burrow in the open clearing to another deeper in the woods. The older and fatter woodchucks start first, some before the first frost. Curling up in a tight ball with their forelegs wrapped behind their heads, they go into hibernation. Their breathing drops to once every six minutes, their heartbeat to four a minute, and their temperature as low as 38 degrees Fahrenheit (3.3 degrees Celsius). During hibernation they lose as much as half their weight.

Learning all about woodchucks gave me a better understanding of their habits, but so far I hadn't found any particular benefit accruing from their existence other than providing food for timber rattlers. But when I started reading about woodchuck burrows, I hit pay dirt, so to speak.

The main entrance to the burrow is usually located under a stump, a rock, or a building and is characterized by a mound of dirt. The six- to eight-inch-diameter entrance extends downward two to four feet and then runs parallel to the surface from fifteen to fifty feet with the possibility of several side galleries. There is almost always one, sometimes as many as five, additional entrances that lack soil piles, since they are excavated from within. These serve as escape holes. The nest chamber is fifteen inches in diameter and eight inches high and is lined with vegetable matter. A separate chamber serves as a latrine. Although the woodchuck digs with its front feet and throws the dirt back with its hind, it removes dirt from the tunnel at the main entrance by pushing it forward with the face and chest. A small burrow can be completed in a day, but burrows are constantly being enlarged. In one instance, 716 pounds of dirt were removed in excavating a burrow, and the average is around 400 pounds per burrow. In New York State alone (excluding Manhattan), an estimated 1.6 million tons of earth are moved each year by woodchucks.

Having read this, I realized that I had discovered the major importance of woodchucks: by moving all this soil every year, they were mixing the soil, aerating it, and improving drainage. Woodchucks could be viewed as overgrown earthworms. It was almost an anticlimax to find that woodchuck burrows also serve as homes for other animals. Even while the woodchuck is hibernating, sealed off in a chamber, the remainder of the burrow can harbor a skunk or fox—the former are major consumers of insects, the latter control the populations of mice.

Science had convinced me that I would have to tolerate the woodchuck, and I turned from guns to chicken wire. To prevent him from tunneling under my fence, I used four-foot-wide fencing and bent the bottom foot outward at a ninety-degree angle, holding this foot flat on the ground with rocks. By the time I figured out how to turn corners without cutting the wire, I had mastered origami, but the resulting fence kept the woodchuck from digging underneath where he encountered a vertical barrier. The fence was held up by black-locust poles spaced fifteen feet apart.

I grew vegetables with impunity until the day the broccoli disappeared. I waited and watched and discovered that that fat, short-legged animal had learned to climb the fence, swarming over it as swiftly as a veteran of an obstacle course. I then added electricity—a single wire strung five inches above the ground outside the chicken-wire fence. Black plastic laid on the ground under the wire kept weeds from growing up and short-circuiting it. This electric fence kept the raccoons out of the sweet corn, and it kept the woodchuck at bay, except for the time he tunneled in from some distance away and came up amid the butternut squash. Fencing is never 100 percent effective, but it does reduce the woodchuck damage.

On the other hand, I have several flower gardens that I leave unfenced for appearance's sake. The woodchuck doesn't seem to like flowers as much as vegetables, but I have caught him eating phlox, lupines, and sunflowers in addition to my parsley. That is why I have resolved to educate the woodchuck. Already I have learned that the running and shouting keep me from being angry when I find my parsley plundered. But so far I have no evidence that the woodchuck has learned a thing.

Dung Ho!

The women's team trained on cow chips for the World Championship Buffalo Chip Throwing Contest in Chadron, Nebraska, but found that dried buffalo dung is slightly heavier than dried cow dung. The rules state that the buffalo chip must be at least six inches in diameter and must be thrown without stepping outside an eight-foot circle. How you hold the chip is optional, and there is a difference of opinion among contestants as to how the dung should be flung. The classical style is to hurl it like a discus, but the frisbee throw has recently become a popular alternative. Propelled by a blend of exertion and artistry, the buffalo chips sail down the course falling where they may. Only the farthest of each contestant's two throws is recorded by the judges.

Chadron, Nebraska, is sand hill country, a blend of wheat fields and ranchland. Sparsely populated, there are only 6,500 residents in the town, and scarcely half as many more in the entire county. The Chadron Fur Trade Days held each July are a big event in which fifty competitors arrive to throw buffalo chips. Last year Rod Hanson hurled his chip a mighty 204 feet to win the men's division and become the 1979 World Champion Buffalo Chip Thrower. His closest competitor was Gary Lackey, 22 feet behind. Beth Ryan beat Christy Brown by a foot and a half for the women's title with a throw of 87 feet.

The organizers of the event are proud of their supply of genuine buffalo chips, which they get from the buffalo herd at nearby Fort Robinson State Park. In the arid Nebraska climate the buffalo dung dries out in only a few days, dry enough that some of the chips are bronzed to serve as prizes.

Buffalo (or cow) chip throwing is the only instance I know of where manure spreading has become a sport. Manure spreading attracts flies, most people would say, not spectators. Those who laugh at the idea of throwing dung by hand are unaware of manure's etymology. Combining the Latin words *manus* (hand) and *operare* (to work), both manure and maneuver come from the same Middle French word meaning "to do work by hand." In the fifteenth and sixteenth centuries, the verb manure had a number of meanings, among them to hold, occupy, administer, or manage land. To manure also meant to till or to cultivate and to train through instruction and discipline. More recently it has come to refer to enriching the land with fertilizer, and, as a noun, the word is now synonymous with fertilizer. The English have a host of manures—green manure, mineral manures, artificial manures, and animal manures, but here in the United States manure refers exclusively to animal dung. While it may seem esoteric to become expert at tossing buffalo chips by hand, the contestants in Nebraska can be credited with reviving some of manure's original meaning.

Manure spreading has a slightly less flamboyant but no less enthusiastic following among backyard gardeners. Manure, whether from a horse, cow, sheep, goat, pig, or chicken, is valued both for its nutrient content and its organic matter, although arguments flare over the question of how much nutrient there actually is in manure.

Conflicting figures can be explained by noting that the nutrient content depends on a lot of things—from what went into the animal to how the stuff was stored after it came out. When people ask, John Page, a county extension agent in Vermont, uses the following numbers: twenty pounds of cow manure is equivalent to a pound of 12-3-9 chemical fertilizer, he says. For horse manure, twenty pounds is equivalent to a pound of 14-5-11. Sheep and goat manure figures out to a pound of 19-7-20. Finally, pig and chicken manure are equivalent to a pound of 10-7-8 and 20-16-8, respectively. To be honest, I've never actually met anyone who stopped to compute the nutrient content of the manure they were using; you can't help but notice its smell as you are forking it about, but that's as close an analysis as it usually gets. European immigrants use manure largely because they always have, and others join in because they find it works. Traditionalists use fresh horse manure instead of electric heating cables to warm their hotbeds. Organic gardeners add manure to their compost piles, and many know to mix a shovelful of manure in a bucket of water to make manure tea with which to feed young cucumber vines.

Gardeners are prevented from using more manure to topdress their rhubarb and asparagus not by its origin or even its odor, but by its scarcity. Years ago when every delivery truck was pulled by a horse, the cities were full of stables. Before zoning regulations prohibited the keeping of pigs and chickens, many a sideyard had its resident supplier out back. Now manure is as scarce as buffalo nickels. Finding some takes a little ingenuity. Of course it's easier to find if your friends have riding horses. There aren't many horses left in the city, but one parish priest I know gets his manure from the mounted police stables. In the outskirts of cities there are poultry farms. Thousands of hens in close quarters, with no land on which to spread the byproduct, guarantees a surplus of manure. Growers of exotic vegetables can consider starting with gnu manure, or zebra, or yak. While a few zoos have post-entry quarantines on their animals that prevent them from giving away their dung, most zoos are eager to. Really enthusiastic manure-hunters will follow circus elephants, and a few apartment dwellers may go as far as to take a fresh look at the family guinea pig.

Once a source of manure has been discovered, the less said about it the better. Not because anyone wishes their neighbor's garden ill, but because there's not enough to go around. Information about local sources of manure is shared among close friends like seeds and cuttings, but newcomers can't expect a broadcast of the news.

Urban gardeners aren't the only creatures who find manure in short supply. Their difficulty in obtaining enough of it is shared by a group of scarab beetles, known as dung beetles, who subsist on a diet of dung. The best-known of these is the sacred scarab of Egypt *(Scarabaeus sacer)* a beetle native to the Mediterranean region whose ball of dung was once likened to the sun being pulled across the heavens.

There are dung beetles in the United States, but despite the great bison herds that once roamed the West, their numbers and kinds are few. One hypothesis is that during the last ice age the large herbivores in the United States and their dung beetles went extinct, and the bison precursors that crossed over the Bering Strait didn't bring any beetles with them.

For dung beetle opulence one must visit the savannahs and grasslands of East Africa. Here great herds of grazing animals deposit massive amounts of dung each day, and yet scarcely any remains to be seen. There are so many dung beetles that in certain regions both the growth and reproduction of the beetles are limited by a scarcity of dung. The appearance of each new piece of dung provokes such a mad scramble that even the most ardent gardener would be left breathless. Bernd Heinrich and George Bartholomew, who studied dung beetles in the Tsavo National Park of Kenya, found that a fist-sized lump of elephant dung attracted more than 3,800 night-flying dung beetles in only fifteen minutes. A typical heap of elephant dung, with its football-sized boluses, attracted proportionately more. Within half an hour the pile was reduced to a thinly spread mat of beetles and dung.

Some species of dung beetles simply burrow into the dung and feed. Other species tunnel into the earth beneath or beside the pile of dung and drag bundles of dung into the burrow, some of which they shape into balls. The balls are used to rear young. One egg is laid in each and the larva that hatches derives all its food and water from the dung. A third group of dung beetles also shapes dung into balls, but these are rolled away before being buried. The beetle grasps the ball with its hind legs and pushes it along as it walks backward. *Scarabaeus laevistriatus,* a large dung beetle that weighs as much as ten grams (one-third of an ounce), can fashion a tennis-ball-size sphere out of elephant dung in a little more than a minute and roll it away at speeds up to fourteen meters (forty-six feet) a minute.

Speed is necessary, for competition is intense at the manure pile. Even as the ball is being formed, burrowing dung bettles are trying to invade it. A completed ball must also be defended from conspecifics who find it easier to steal than make one's own. At the approach of another beetle, the ball roller moves to position himself between the attacker and the ball and tries to keep rolling. If the attacker succeeds in climbing onto the ball, a fight ensues, both beetles hanging onto the dung ball with their middle and hind legs while battering one another with their powerful forelegs. The loser is often thrown ten centimeters (four inches) or more through the air. The human analogy would be two gardeners punching each other in combat over a wheelbarrow of cow manure.

All of this dung beetle activity means that the ground is kept clear of dung. The beetles also fertilize and aerate the soil by burying the dung, they reduce the spread of parasites and disease, and they reduce the numbers of flies. These are among the reasons that Australia wanted some African dung beetles. Until 1788, Australia didn't need African dung beetles: none of the native animals produced dung larger than a golf ball, and about 250 species of well-adapted native beetles dispersed it. But the first English colonists brought with them five cows, two bulls, seven horses, and forty-four sheep. Since then, the animals, as well as the colonists, have increased. Cows drop about twelve dung pads a day, and six million of these are now falling on Australia every half hour.

In Africa these meadow muffins disappear in minutes, but in Australia the cow pads were lasting for months and even years until they finally disintegrated as a result of trampling, weathering, or termite attack. Where the dry cow chips lay no grass grew and Australia was losing six million acres of pasture a year. In 1963, D. F. Waterhouse and other scientists decided to import a range of dung beetles from Africa in an attempt to control the cow dung that was overwhelming Australia. After transplanting African dung beetle eggs into Australian cow-dung balls to avoid importing disease that might be present in the African dung, several species were released in 1967. The results have been most satisfactory. In many parts of Australia dung pads are now rapidly eliminated. The annual savings are in the hundreds of thousands of dollars. The only complaint, according to Waterhouse, came from a cattle raiser who objected that he could no longer find cow chips with which to level his irrigation pipes and had to carry wooden blocks instead.

Until the dung beetle was introduced, commercial agriculture in Australia was suffering from a layer of dung spread thinly across the continent. In the United States the problem is enormous concentrations of manure. Beef cattle are raised on pasture until they reach 50 or 60 percent of full weight, and then they are moved to feedlots. When there are 100,000 beef cattle all in one place, all being fed corn, hay, and silage plentifully, the most conspicuous result is manure, a mountain of it. Modern dairies have the same problem—with as many as 2,500 cows, each giving more manure than milk. All over the country animal production has become centralized. The density of animals has increased far beyond the carrying capacity of the site, and food for the animals must be imported by truck and rail from great distances. Whereas it was once relatively easy to load the manure into a manure spreader and drive around the adjoining fields to dispose of it, the adjoining fields would now be smothered by the huge amounts. Until recently the manure coming out of these meat and milk factories was just allowed to pile up, eventually draining into streams and lakes. Now strict regulations promulgated by the Environmental Protection Agency are aimed at preventing such pollution. Agricultural engineers are calculating the biological oxygen demand of various kinds of manure and designing water-tight lagoon storage systems. Everyone wants the nutrients to end up back on the land where they came from, but no one seems sure just how to get them there.

Engineers with their computer programs for mechanized manure-handling systems may come up with a technologically sophisticated way to get manure back to the land, but if they fail they might consider the home gardener. The home gardener and the African dung beetle have a lot in common. Australia capitalized on the voracity of dung beetles. American livestock producers might consider using the manure-gathering propensity of the small gardener. There are, after all, millions of them. Some carry manure off in garbage bags and trash cans, others are capable of hauling away whole truckloads. Gardeners transport the manure to agricultural land where it is carefully worked into the ground, fertilizing and aerating the soil, reducing the spread of parasites and disease and reducing the number of flies.

I can envision the discovery of each new mountain of manure. The air would ring with cries of "dung ho!" as hordes of gardeners swept down upon it armed with shovels and manure forks. Within hours the pile would be gone, rolling away toward small gardens in microbuses, pickup trucks and wheelbarrows. It would be a sight better than buffalo chip throwing.

The Attraction
of Wild Bees

The neighbors are building birdhouses in hopes of attracting insect-feeding wrens, purple martins, and blue-birds to their gardens this summer. I am busy building bee houses. These are not to be mistaken for beehives. A bee-hive is a structure in which you keep bees that you already own. Each of my wooden boxes is intended to attract a wild swarm of honeybees, and in a sense they differ as much from beehives as birdhouses differ from chicken coops.

My interest in bees comes from an interest in melons. Melon vines have separate male and female flowers, and unless a bee transfers pollen from the stamens of the male flowers to the stigmas of the female flowers, there will be no warm, fragrant, and fragile muskmelons to eat on an August afternoon. Bees also make honey from the nectar they collect, but this is of secondary interest to a true melon fancier. Having a large number of bees ready and waiting for each five-petaled, yellow blossom to open helps assure a good crop of the sweet, netted globes. For many people this is more than enough justification for keeping a colony of bees next to the garden.

The usual way to obtain a colony of honeybees is to order a screen box from a southern apiary. Inside will be 3 pounds of honeybees (approximately 3,500 bees per pound) and a fertile queen, her majesty safely imprisoned in a tiny wood-and-screen box of her own. These packaged bees become more expensive every year, while the price of wild honeybee swarms stays the same. They are free.

Honeybee colonies multiply by swarming. A swarm is simply a large group of bees in search of a new nest site. Within established colonies new queens are reared each spring, the grublike larvae occupying large peanut-shaped cells on the surface of the regular comb of hexagonal cells. These larvae are fed nothing but royal jelly, and it is this special diet that makes them grow into queens rather than sterile workers. When the queen cells are capped with wax to permit the larvae to metamorphose into adult queen bees, the colony swarms. The old queen leaves the nest accompanied by nearly half the workers, never knowing which of the new queens will ultimately become her successor.

From outside the nest the sight is spectacular, a torrent of bees launching into flight as ten thousand pour out of the entrance. For a few moments they fill the sky, and then drawing mysteriously together, they settle, forming a golden-brown cluster draped over a tree branch or massed on the side of a building. The porcupine-size ball is solid bees, each worker bee gripping onto the bee next to her, all of them attracted by a chemical secreted by the queen in their midst.

From the swarm, scouts fly off in search of a new nest site. Successful scouts return to the swarm and signal the location of their discovery with a waggle dance similar to the one they use to indicate the location of a new food source. Several possible nest sites may be considered, other scout bees flying off to inspect each of them. When a majority of dancers signal for a certain site, the swarm flies off to occupy it just as suddenly as it left the parent colony. The entire process, from the time the swarm leaves the parent colony until it settles in a new nest, may take a few minutes or a few days.

Whether the swarm originated from an apiary or a wild colony, once it has left the parent colony, it is effectively wild. If you can capture a swarm before it moves into a new nest, you will have yourself a colony of bees. Sometimes the swarms are very conspicuous, surrounded by police, firefighters, and frightened bystanders. Perhaps it is fear of massive numbers of stings, anaphalactic shock, or Brazilian "killer" bees that upsets people. Some people may be unnerved simply by the altruistic way in which a worker bee so readily gives up her life by stinging.

These fears are all groundless, for honeybees in a swarm are unusually docile. As long as the swarm is clustered in the open, the bees almost never sting. You can even reach into a swarm of bees with your bare hand, scoop out a handful, and throw it. The bee ball holds together for a few yards, then the bees scatter and fly back to the swarm.

Whenever a swarm is sighted, beekeepers are glad to come to the rescue of the community for they get a free colony of bees and a chance to be heroic with little effort. The mock heroism is called "grandstanding," and the effect is enhanced by wearing a suit and tie and nonchalantly collecting the swarm in a used cardboard box. Later the bees can be dumped into an empty beehive, where they will begin keeping hive at once.

Most swarms of bees are not collected by beekeepers, however. Bee swarms have been escaping from domestic colonies into the wild ever since honeybees were first brought to this country from Europe in the early 1600s. The swarms move into hollow trees, creating bee trees whose sweet stores are sought by a few patient and persistent bee hunters. Where buildings are abundant, the bees may occupy chimneys or spaces within the walls of houses. In agricultural areas where beekeepers have hives but trees are scarce, many of the swarms that escape probably perish for want of a suitable nest site. A swarm that cannot find a new nest will begin to construct combs in the open and will remain on them throughout the summer, but winter weather in the north always proves fatal.

Gardeners do not have the time to chase about the countryside collecting bee swarms, even if the resulting colonies are free. I'm planning to retire from the activity myself and spend more time with the plants. This is why I am building bee houses—so I can collect swarms of bees automatically. Although I already have several hives of bees, the result of past swarm chasing, an occasional colony dies out during the winter, and I need a new swarm to replace it.

My new bee houses are technically called bait hives, and they are the by-products of basic research into honeybee biology. As a graduate student at Harvard, Tom Seeley wanted to find out what qualities the scout bees were looking for when they evaluated a potential nest site. He experimented with a variety of wooden containers in different locations, watching to see which ones were chosen first by honeybee swarms. He discovered that the bees prefer a preformed cavity with a 40-liter volume that is located high off the ground. The preferred nest site also has a small, south-facing entrance located at the bottom of the cavity.

From his discovery came the plans for a bait hive. Each bait hive measures 14 × 15 × 15 inches. They are made of five-eighth-inch plywood tightly joined at the corners. The back panel is longer than the others, giving a flange to nail through when attaching the bait hive to a tree. (If you use double-headed nails, it will be easier to remove the hive when the time comes to transfer the bees to a permanent home.) The bottom of the bait hive, held in place by eye-hooks, is removable to facilitate cleaning. At the lower edge of the front is a circular hole, one and one-quarter inch in diameter, with a nail bent across it to prevent the bee house from becoming a birdhouse. I have also painted the bait hives green to protect them from weather and target practice by hunters.

Swarming season here in the Northeast is from May to July, and I will nail the boxes high up in a conspicuous location on the south side of trees before the season begins. Although the bait hives should be clearly visible, it is best if they are shaded from above. I don't expect to capture swarms in all the bait hives, but Tom Seeley and his colleague Roger Morse from Cornell found that in upstate New York, 50 percent of their bait hives were colonized by swarms each year.

Bees flying regularly in and out of the bait hive will indicate that a swarm has moved in. At this point one can simply leave the bait hive where it is. The bees who have already begun building wax combs in it will go on occupying the box just as they would a hollow tree. There are, however, several disadvantages to leaving the bees in the bait hive. Unless it is very well built, the bait hive may not withstand year after year of weathering, and you won't be able to remove any of the honey without destroying the colony. Finally the USDA bee inspectors won't approve of leaving bees in the bait hive, as you are not supposed to keep bees in hives that cannot be inspected for disease.

Bee houses aren't bee hives, but the simplest way to avoid any possible confrontation on the subject is to transfer the bees to a standard beehive. This involves climbing up to the bait hive at night when all the bees have retired and covering the entrance hole with a piece of screen. Next, detach the bait hive from the tree.

In the morning, lay the bait hive on its back so that the entrance faces upward and remove the screen. At this point several angry bees will come flying out of the entrance and you should be prepared to become a beekeeper. Either you have a tolerance for occasional stings or you are wearing the jumpsuit, gauntlet gloves, and a veil to prevent them. You will need an empty beehive and an acquaintance with its components. First, lay an inner cover on top of the bait hive so that the entrance hole in the bait hive lines up with the hole in the center of the inner cover. Next, place a hive body containing ten frames with beeswax foundation on top of the inner cover. Finally, invert a bottom board and place it on top of the hive body. This will provide a new entrance for the bees. In a sense, you have simply turned a beehive upside down and positioned it on top of the bait hive.

Next drill a one-half-inch hole into the side of the bait hive and, with a smoker, blow smoke into the bait hive, driving the bees up into the new hive body. When most of the bees have crawled up, slip a queen excluder in between the inner cover and the hive body to prevent the queen from returning to the combs in the bait hive and laying more eggs.

Leave the bait hive and the beehive attached in this way for three weeks until all the larvae in the bait hive have matured into adult bees. Then separate the two, rearranging the beehive components so that the bottom board is on the bottom, the inner and an outer cover on the top. The bait hive can be stored until next season. Leave the combs inside, because they will make the bait hive more attractive for swarms next year, but you should cover the entrance to prevent wax moths from getting in and laying eggs, because the larvae will destroy the combs.

You don't have to be interested in keeping bees yourself to set out bait hives. You will find that almost any beekeeper will be glad to have the swarms you collect. You can offer to trade swarms in return for the beekeeper's leaving a hive of bees near your garden for the season.

By building bait hives you may be helping to conserve

populations of wild honeybees, just as the construction of nest boxes rescued the wood duck from its rapid decline in numbers. By approximating the ideal hollow tree, bait hives provide honeybee swarms with a preferred nest site where land clearing or tree surgery has deprived them of natural cavities.

Rarely does conservation offer gardeners such immediate rewards. The bees will quickly improve the yields of many fruits and vegetables, and anyone who remains skeptical about the value of their presence will be convinced by the strong, pungent ambrosia of a vine-ripened muskmelon.

Duckweed

A green scum coats the small farm pond, a verdant film spread across the water from the sedges on one side to the cattails on the other. Close up, the scum resolves into millions of individual plants, minute free-floating duckweeds, dividing and growing so rapidly that they threaten to crowd out even the frogs floating in their midst. The pond water in which these sequin-size aquatic plants are growing is rich with manure and other fertilizers washed by rain from the adjoining field. With ample nutrients, full sun, and protection from the wind, the duckweed population is growing exponentially, the individual plants piling up on top of one another to form a crust that is already half an inch thick.

The midmorning summer calm of this pond is interrupted by the arrival of a ten-year-old boy who hikes across the weedy dam and out onto the dock. He carries a long bamboo fishing pole, for the pond is stocked with black bass. Squatting, he breaks off the mummified remains of the last worm from the hook and baits it with a fresh one. Then after unwinding the line from around the pole, he stands and swings the line with its red-and-white plastic bobber out into the pond. The bobber plops into the duckweed followed by the worm, but both remain on the surface. Only after adding a lead sinker does the hook have enough weight to break through the floating mat. Even then when he lifts up the line to inspect the bait, he finds it plastered with duckweed. Discouraged, the boy gathers in the line and walks away.

The next afternoon he is back with his fishing pole and a makeshift sieve made from old window screening and the grill from a large chicken feeder. By using the sieve to skim duckweed off the surface, he collects a great heap of it on the dock, but like oil the remaining plants simply spread out to cover the surface once more.

The boy's final idea is to equip one of his grandmother's cows with an inner tube around each leg and push it off the dock. The cow could then float around, feed on the duckweed, and clear the surface for fishing. But his grandmother, on whose farm the pond is located, won't let him borrow a cow.

This duckweed, which is such a hindrance to summer angling, is something of a curiosity to botanists. Of the three hundred thousand or so known flowering plants, duckweed in the smallest and simplest. The plants have no distinct leaves or stems; instead the two are united into a single, more or less oval frond, which is sometimes called a thallus, and which floats on or just beneath the surface of fresh water. Most duckweeds have no roots, and those that do have only short, unbranched rootlets hanging down from the fronds. Botanists consider the duckweed family, the Lemnaceae, to be a close relative of the aroid family and explain the peculiar simplicity of the duckweeds as an evolutionary reduction of all those structures not absolutely necessary for life on the surface of a freshwater pond.

Wherever the water is warm enough for swimming, there are species of duckweeds—thirty species in all, distributed worldwide and divided into six genera. *Spirodela* contains the largest plants. *Spirodela polyrhiza,* the great duckweed, is a mighty three-eighths of an inch long. Duckweeds in the genera *Lemna, Pseudowolffia Wolffiella,* and *Wolffiopsis* are even smaller, many of them only one-sixteenth of an inch long. But the blue ribbon for minuteness among flowering plants goes to species of *Wolffia.* These plants are so small that they have earned the common name watermeal, for they look like grains of green flour sprinkled on the water's surface. *Wolffia microscopica* from India is aptly named: full-grown plants are scarcely one-thirty-second of an inch long. Four of them would fit comfortably on the head of a pin.

With fronds scarcely visible as individual plants, duckweeds might easily be mistaken for algae. But duckweeds do have flowers, although they are just as simple as the plants. While the flowers have no petals, in some species there is an aroidlike spathe that encloses the flowers temporarily. The flowers are unisexual, the male flowers having one or, rarely, two stamens, the female flower only a single pistil. Not only are the flowers minute, they are rare. It is safe to say that more fishermen have seen the Loch Ness monster than have ever seen duckweeds in bloom.

Since flowering is rare and fruiting even more so, duckweeds rely on a different form of reproduction to achieve such rapid population growth. Their principal means of reproduction is by asexual budding. Each frond of *Lemna* has two regions of actively dividing cells that alternately produce new fronds. A single frond may produce as many as twenty offspring before it dies. Although new fronds may remain attached to the parent plant for a brief time, they ultimately break free to float independently. Many duckweeds can double their numbers in under three days. If you were to place a single square inch of *Lemna minor,* the common duckweed, into a suitable pond, at the end of two months duckweed would completely cover five acres of water. Corn is one of the most rapidly growing terrestrial plants; yet the subtropical duckweed *Lemna paucicosta* has a relative growth rate nearly fourteen times as great. The floating nature of the duckweed plant is partly responsible for this magic-beanstalklike growth. With no woody tissue needed for support, virtually the entire plant is involved in photosynthesis. Growth results in additional plants that break away, assuring that every plant retains a constant relationship with the environment. Finally, because the duckweeds have no attachment to the soil, they are unaffected by changes in the water level.

All of this culminates in the thick green scum of tiny plants that can ruin summer fishing. The scum can also clog irrigation pumps, foul small hydroelectric facilities, and make it difficult for livestock to drink. Duckweed is too small to kill by mowing or crushing, and efforts at controlling its growth have largely involved chemical herbicides. Many of these are less than ideal because they may render the water unsuitable for such uses as drinking or irrigation. Perhaps the most imaginative, and least effective, control technique was practiced by the elderly gentleman who walked to the edge of his pond each afternoon and chipped duckweed out of it with his golf club. If the plant is so hard to eradicate, why not find a use for it? In the case of duckweed, this is easy. Not only is duckweed one of the most vigorous of all plants, but it proves to be highly nutritious. The crude protein content of dried *Spirodela oligorhiza* averages nearly 40 percent, more than twice that of the best alfalfa. Furthermore, duckweed protein has higher percentages of lysine and arginine (two amino acids important in animal feeds) than does alfalfa. In terms of yield per acre, a duckweed pond produces two and a half times as much protein per acre as the best alfalfa pasture, and ten times as much as a soybean field.

Duckweeds are relished by herbivorous fish and wild fowl (including ducks), and in tropical Africa, India, and Southeast Asia, duckweeds are harvested for pig feed. In Burma, Laos, and northern Thailand, *Wolffia arrhiza* is eaten as a vegetable. Called *khai-nam,* meaning eggs-of-the-water, it is cultivated in rain-fed pools; the thick yellow green mats that form are harvested every three to four days. From each square yard of pond, about a pound and a half of fresh duckweed is gathered each week, a yield much greater than that from any of their other vegetable crops.

To top it all off, duckweed is an excellent cattle feed.

Not long ago, in *American Scientist* (July–August 1978), William Hillman, a plant physiologist, and Dudley Culley, Jr., an aquaculture specialist, outlined plans for a duckweed/dairy farm. Their scheme capitalizes on the rapid growth of duckweed in ponds that have been enriched by barnyard nutrients.

Their proposed farm has an average-size herd of one hundred cows and, in theory, operates as follows. In addition to milk, the cows produce a great deal of manure—some 4.5 tons per day. The manure is first pumped to a fermentation unit, where methane is generated and the volume is reduced by 50 percent. The residue is then pumped to a series of lagoons totaling ten acres. The lagoons are only three feet deep, and they are equipped with skimmers to harvest the duckweed. The authors calculate that the total yield of these lagoons will be 4.8 tons of fresh duckweed per day. Once the water has been drained off, the duckweed is mixed with other feed. It will provide roughly 20 percent of each cow's daily food intake (in terms of dry weight) and 60 percent of each cow's daily protein requirement. If more duckweed were available, more could be fed to the cows, since experiments have shown that cows can consume 75 percent of their diet in duckweed with no ill effects.

In the tropics and subtropics, duckweed grows year-round, but in the Temperate Zone the yield will be severely reduced in winter months. Methods are therefore being devised for solar drying and storage of duckweed for winter feeding.

Finally, duckweed might be used to salvage chemicals from industrial waste water. *Lemna minor* and *L. trisulca* concentrate ten times more boron than do other aquatic plants. *Lemna minor* collected from the America River in California contained concentrations of aluminum 660,000 times greater than the water it was growing in. The plants also contained high levels of manganese, iron, titanium, copper, and cobalt.

Someday we may see a great many more small ponds covered with a green scum, the duckweeds feeding on water rich with animal manures and human sewage. In the laboratory, strains of duckweed have been found to reproduce as often as every sixteen hours. Under ideal growing conditions, small ponds may yield enormous amounts of plant matter, in an easily processed form, that can be used to feed both animals and people. But if they are going to give out awards for the idea that duckweed should be fed to cows, I want one. I thought of it twenty years ago, but no one would lend me a cow.

Zeus and
the Ash Tree

M y curiosity about lightning is tempered by a re-luctance to be electrocuted. Ben Franklin, after all, was lucky that lightning did not strike his kite, but even his discovery that lightning is a powerful electrical discharge has not deterred others from seeking to study it firsthand. In 1930, Professor R. W. Woods of Johns Hopkins University chastised a cook for running away from an unusual form of lightning called ball lightning. "The cook was near enough to the ball to touch it, and it is regrettable," he wrote, "that she neglected the opportunity of making a valuable contribution to our knowledge of this mysterious electrical phenomenon!" I admire the professor's spirit of scientific inquiry, but I question his approach.

It is due to the efforts of similarly dedicated lightning bugs that we have a good, although still incomplete, understanding of lightning. We know that most lightning is the result of a separation of electric charges within thunderclouds, although the cause of the separation is still under debate. The bottom of the cloud becomes negatively charged with a surplus of electrons, while both the top of the cloud and the ground are positively charged. When the difference in charge between the ground and the negatively charged bottom of the cloud becomes great enough, electrons plunge to earth forming a lightning bolt several thousand feet long.

Sir Charles Boys invented a special camera in 1902 for photographing the movements of a single lightning bolt and spent thirty years trying unsuccessfully to take pictures with it. Others, however, have used a modified Boys camera to prove that lightning bolts are made up of two stages. The first is a weakly luminous "leader" that advances toward the ground in a series of 150-foot "steps." When the leader contacts the ground, it is followed by the second stage, a much brighter "return stroke" as electrons drain out of the column from the bottom. Since the typical stepped leader moves earthward at 93 miles per second, and the return stroke moves upward at 31,000 miles per second, the lightning bolt appears as a single bright flash to the human eye. Occasionally, you may see lightning flicker. These are multiple strokes occurring within a single lightning bolt.

Personally, I shy away from electric fences that contain only a few thousand volts, so the thought of the one hundred million volts contained in a lightning bolt leaves me content to lie in bed at night during thunderstorms, counting the number of seconds between the flash and the rumble of the thunder to determine how far away the lightning streak was (five seconds equals one mile). But recently the lightning has been striking closer to home. A white ash tree next to the house now has a twelve-inch-wide barkless scar starting at the topmost branch and running all the way down to the roots. Across the road a red pine was killed so quickly that the needles were left brown and hanging on the tree.

Golfers and church steeples get lots of publicity when they are struck by lightning, but trees are the most common targets. Most lightning passes through trees on the way to the ground, because water is a better electrical conductor than air. Unfortunately, the water in a tree is concentrated near the cambium just under the bark. As the electricity from the lightning surges through this water, it causes it to boil explosively, blasting off the bark, sometimes throwing pieces of it a hundred feet or more.

A typical lightning bolt contains 250 kilowatt hours of electricity, not nearly as much as most people think, but producing enough energy to lift the S.S. *United States* out of the water. What makes lightning exceptionally destructive is its short duration. "Cold" bolts are characterized by high electrical current and extremely short duration. One of these penetrating to the heart of a tree can convert it instantaneously to kindling. "Hot" bolts are of lower electrical current but slightly longer duration. They are likely to set things on fire. Each year about 7,500 forest fires are started by lightning in the United States.

I am not so worried about starting a forest fire, because here in the East thunderstorms are usually accompanied by heavy rains that quench any fire that breaks out. I am more concerned about the destruction of venerable shade trees near the house. Some of these trees are more than a hundred years old, and their shade could not be replaced in my lifetime. A tree doesn't have to be destroyed instantly to be killed by lightning. Death may take several years. The ash tree that was struck is still alive, but its long, open wound is an invitation to insects and fungi, and I am afraid that the tree will ultimately succumb to this injury. To protect the other trees from a similar fate, I resolved to install lightning rods. The lightning rod is a simple device, and as effective at protecting ash trees as it is at protecting barns. The metal of the lightning rod provides an even better conductor than the moisture in the trunk, so the lightning bolt is guided down to earth without injuring the tree.

It was impractical to put a rod in every tree, so I first tried to find out whether certain tree species were more likely to be struck. In the library I found various studies that recorded the numbers and species of trees struck by lightning, but in most of these the investigators had failed to record the frequency with which each species occurred in the forest, so it was impossible to calculate a relative susceptibility to lightning.

A German study done by Lippe in 1889 did record both the struck and the unstruck trees in 50,000 acres of forest. Although 70 percent of the trees in the forest were beech, only 6 percent of the trees struck by lightning were beech. Oaks, on the other hand, made up only 11 percent of the forest but 58 percent of the trees struck by lightning. From this Lippe concluded that oaks were sixty-two times more likely to be struck than beech. Subsequent microscopic study of beech wood has shown that it contains large amounts of oil, which is a poor conductor of electricity. The wood of oaks, by contrast, has a high water content.

Smooth-barked trees like the beech may be less damaged by lightning even when they are struck, for rainwater on a smooth-barked tree forms a continuous sheet down which electricity can flow without harming the internal tissues of the tree. There may be some scorching, bark furrowing, or killing of small branches, but no deep-seated splitting of the bole.

The species of the tree may not be as important as how tall or how isolated it is. Even the type of soil that the tree is growing on seems to affect its probability of being struck. I could find no sure way to predict which tree will be selected by a lightning bolt.

Faced with this, I simply chose the tallest trees that were closest to the house. Each lightning rod provides a "cone of protection" around it, a region extending horizontally from the tree base roughly the height of the lightning rod. Within this cone, lightning bolts will be drawn to the rod and won't damage other buildings or trees.

Elegant lightning rods have a copper or brass spike attached to the top of a three-eighth-inch copper cable extending down into the ground. But the price of copper has gone up even faster than that of hamburger, and I turned to steel as a substitute. Galvanized pipe is not as good a conductor as copper, but by increasing the diameter, the conductance becomes equivalent. One-inch galvanized pipe is a lot cheaper than copper, and a lot less attractive to the free-lance copper miners who have begun to frequent these parts. I bought pipe in fifteen-foot sections, carried them up into the tree one at a time, and connected them together with pipe fittings. The topmost pipe stuck up several feet above the topmost twigs, and before I screwed it in place, I added a sharpened steel spike to its end. The entire column of pipe I tied loosely to the tree trunk with nylon rope. All lightning rods must have adequate ground connections so that the electricity is dispersed into the earth. I connected the bottom of the pipe with one-half-inch copper tubing to several half-inch copper-covered steel ground rods driven a full eight feet into the ground. It is best to pound these in at a distance from the trunk to prevent the electricity that runs down them from damaging the roots.

If the tree is still growing, you will have to climb up after a few years and add a section of pipe. I have had to climb up and loosen the nylon ropes so that they don't cut into the trunk.

I'm not sure whether any of my lightning rods have been struck in the five years that they have been up, but no more trees have been damaged. The probability that any tall object will be struck by lightning depends on both its height and the number of thunderstorms each year. Calculations on an isolated seventy-five-foot-tall object on level ground show that it will be struck once every three years if there are thirty thunderstorm days per year, about what we have here in New Hampshire. In regions where there is twice as much lightning, a tree will be struck twice as often, just as it will if it is twice as tall.

I expect the lightning rods to continue to protect the trees that they are installed in, but I can't make any guarantee about the other trees, even those within the cone of protection. Lightning has a capricious quality that bedevils prediction. Calculating what will be struck, how often, and with what effect is quite impossible. This unpredictability combined with the destructive power of lightning has understandably spawned legends.

If the ash tree with its trunk-length scar eventually dies, I shall have to saw it down. The Thompson Indians from British Columbia would then advise me to use the wood to make incendiary arrows, since they believe such arrows will be more destructive than ordinary ones. I am more likely to burn the wood in the stove, ignoring the Wendish peasants of Saxony who fear that this will make my house catch fire. I would hope that the tribesmen of Northern Rhodesia are right, that burning such wood will give me physical and spiritual benefits.

The ancient Greeks thought lightning bolts were forged by the lame blacksmith Hephaestus and hurled by Zeus as an expression of his displeasure. Some of this legend has given way to facts. We know now that lightning is produced by the separation of electric charges within thunderclouds, but we still don't know why it strikes the objects it does, and I am left wondering what the ash tree next to the house could possibly have done that upset Zeus.

In the Night Garden

The flower garden at night is an exotic spot, where an odor, a sound, or a light may signal an enemy, a meal, or a mate. It is virtually unexplored, though, for gardeners like other people are accustomed to daylight vision, and rarely go abroad in the dark without a streetlight or other artificial illumination. Instead they wait indoors, imagining hordes of rabbits, woodchucks, and slugs rampaging through the shadows. But those willing to go on a sensual journey will venture into the garden after dark, receptive to the scents, sounds, and sights of an unfamiliar place.

At first the night garden is invisible. Stepping outdoors from a well-lit house leaves you blind, afraid to move for fear of stumbling over the wheelbarrow. But during the next twenty to forty minutes your eyes will adapt to the darkness, becoming ten thousand times more sensitive. Starlight, which provides only one billionth as much light as clear daylight at noon, becomes sufficient for distinguishing various objects. The brick walk, the flowers, the garden bench have no color. Everything appears in black and white, a property of the dark-adapted eye. For at such low light levels only the black and white receptors in the human eye, called rods, are active. The cones, sensitive to color, are not, and hence night vision is color blind. The increased sensitivity of the rod system after half an hour in the dark comes in part from the resynthesis of a pigment called rhodopsin, or visual purple, which has been bleached by bright light. Vitamin A is an ingredient of rhodopsin, and such vitamin A–yielding foods as carrots do improve your ability to see in the dark.

Once your eyes are adapted to the dark, you can begin to observe the flowers. The most conspicuous ones are those which are white by day. Many of these open at night and release a heavy sweet perfume that contrasts with the cool night air. Night-blooming white flowers such as nicotiana, angel's-trumpet *(Datura inoxia)*, the plantain lily *(Hosta plantaginea)*, and the moonflower vine *(Ipomoea alba)* have been popular for a long time, entire gardens being planted exclusively to white flowers for nighttime enjoyment.

The behavior of flowers at night has an ecological basis. It is linked to the daily rhythm of their pollinators. Thus the flowers that open at night do so because it is then that pollinating moths are active. The moths and the plants have evolved in response to each other, structure and behavior becoming synchronized to facilitate the exchange of nectar in return for the transfer of pollen by the moth.

Moths are attracted to the deeply lobed petals of white flowers as well as by their strong night scent. Whether alighting on the flower to feed, or hovering in front of it as the large hawk moths do, the moth uses its long thin proboscis to probe deep into the tube or spur of the flower where the nectar is secreted. Its appetite only partially satisfied by this meal of nectar, the moth flies to another flower, unintentionally transferring pollen from one flower to another. The entire scene—the sweet air, the white flowers against a black background, a scattering of moths—is a ghostly transfiguration of the daytime display.

If you watch a particular moth, you may see it suddenly veer away. The darkness which obscures the moth to human eyes offers the moth virtually no protection from the little brown myotis bats that hunt in the air above the garden. These bats can locate even small insects in complete darkness with a system of ultrasonic echolocation, transmitting short bursts of sound, each with a frequency that drops from 100,000 to 30,000 cycles per second. At the mercy of such a system it is surprising that moths ever escape. But although the human ear cannot hear sound above 23,000 cycles per second, noctuid moths, common nocturnal pollinators, have ears located on the sides of the thorax which are sensitive to the entire range of the bat's signal and are maximally sensitive to frequencies between 15,000 and 60,000 cycles per second. Evolution has thus provided the moth with an early warning device. The moth can detect a hunting bat a hundred feet away and responds by veering away from the source of the sound. Should the bat somehow get within twenty feet, the moth takes violent evasive action, folding its wings and dropping, power-diving, or flying erratically.

Our senses do not permit us to hear the bat's approach, but we can readily perceive the nocturnal courtship of fireflies. These little beetles have solved the problem of communicating in the absence of light by producing their own. Each species has a specific flash pattern that it uses to identify itself to a potential mate. The male *Photinus pyralis,* for instance, flies in an undulating pattern, emitting half-second flashes, each of which makes a **J** of yellow green light. Should the male pass within a few feet of a female waiting on the ground or on a plant in the garden, she responds with a flash of her own two seconds later. The male then flies in her direction and flashes again. She responds, he responds, he locates her, and they then mate.

With our limited senses, we can only share a portion of the night garden's activity. We can smell the flowers, hear the crickets, feel the mosquitos, and see the flash of the fireflies. We cannot sense the chemical plume of sex attractant from female moths calling mates, or the brief bursts of sound from bats seeking prey. But a journey into the night garden is an opportunity to awake the senses we have, and to marvel at how the setting of the sun changes a familiar garden into another land full of intricate and strange exchanges.

The Fungus Connection

The beauty of woodland wildflowers is that they exist at all. Finding a painted trillium or a pink lady's slipper elicits exclamations of admiration, as much from surprise that such a delicate flower is thriving unattended as from an appreciation of its form or color. Garden columbines and lilies rival wildflowers in appearance, but one need only reflect upon the amount of weeding, staking, and fertilizing needed to assure a crop of cultivated blossoms to marvel at the survival of their wild relatives.

Deep in the woods, the sunlight reaches the ground only in tiny spots, and these move continuously across the forest floor. The only soil nutrients are those that have escaped the net of tree roots. Voracious slugs, caterpillars, and warm-blooded beasts wander freely in search of a meal. In the face of such obstacles, it is not surprising that many wildflowers are rare. What is surprising is that they are not extinct. The species that continue to thrive in the shadowy recesses of the forest have obviously evolved means to escape predators, avoid competition, and obtain enough energy for growth.

In the half-light of the forest floor, the energy problem is the easiest to appreciate. Sunlight is essential for photosynthesis. Without it, plants cannot synthesize the high-energy carbohydrates from carbon dioxide and water. Some woodland wildflowers, which live beneath deciduous trees, complete their season's photosynthesis early in the spring before the trees leaf out, while others have evolved the ability to carry on the necessary photosynthesis at low light levels throughout the summer. However, several species of wildflowers that can grow in the deep shade of evergreen forests have taken the unanticipated step of giving up photosynthesis altogether and no longer need even the small amount of sunlight that reaches them. Such extreme behavior is exhibited by the Indian pipe and the pinesap.

On a midsummer walk through a northern conifer forest, you may suddenly come upon a clump of white, waxy stems, each less than a foot tall, lined with small scalelike bracts and topped by a single nodding flower. The combined shape of the stem and flower have given the plant the name Indian pipe. It is as delicate as its appearance: the plant cannot be handled, for the slightest bruise will cause the translucent tissue to blacken. It takes only a week or so for the stems to rise to their full height. When the flowers are pollinated, they rotate to face upward, and then the entire plant shrivels and blackens. The plant's ephemeral nature and its funereal pallor have earned it two additional common names: corpse plant and ghost plant.

The Indian pipe's Latin name is *Monotropa uniflora,* the

first half of the name coming from a Greek word meaning "having a single turn," because the summit of the stem is turned to one side thus causing the single flower to nod. Botanists are unsure of what family to place *Monotropa* in. Some of them, eagerly seizing on the fact that *Monotropa* has no chlorophyll, have created a special family, the Monotropaceae. More temperate taxonomists put *Monotropa* in the family Pyrolaceae, along with pipsissewa and pyrola. Both of these families are extremely close to the heath family, the Ericaceae. Indeed, some botanists would lump them all together into one family.

Slightly less common than the Indian pipe is the pinesap, *Monotropa hypopitys.* There is no disagreement over the common name, but some authorities prefer to put pinesap into a separate genus, in which case it is called *Hypopitys monotropa.* Pinesap differs from Indian pipe in having more than one flower atop each stem. In addition, although there are whitish plants, most pinesaps are yellow, tan, or reddish. They may occur alongside Indian pipe but more commonly grow in slightly drier soils.

Both Indian pipe and pinesap have no chlorophyll and as such cannot synthesize their own food as normal plants can. Clearly these two wildflowers have evolved a means to obtain food from elsewhere, but how do they do it?

An initially attractive theory is that *Monotropa* is a parasite just like broomrape *(Orobanche)* and beechdrops *(Epifagus).* Indeed, early investigators concluded that the roots of the *Monotropa* were penetrating into the food-conducting tissues of the roots belonging to their chlorophyll-possessing neighbors. Unfortunately this has proved to be incorrect. As early as 1826, more thorough investigation showed that although the roots of *Monotropa* were thoroughly mixed with tree roots in the soil, the roots of the wildflower did not penetrate into the roots of the trees.

The alternative explanation for the survival of Indian pipe and pinesap is that the plants are saprophytes; that is, they feed on dead organic matter absorbing preexisting carbohydrates directly from the soil as do certain fungi and bacteria. With the demise of the *Monotropa*-as-parasite theory, the saprophyte theory became widely accepted. It was bolstered by the discovery that the roots of *Monotropa* are completely encased in a layer of fungus. This fungus, a species of *Boletus,* spreads a mantle of fungal mycelia over the roots, and it was suggested that the fungus might help with the absorption of carbohydrates. This fungal association is essential, for although pinesap seeds will germinate, the seedlings will not grow until the fungus has become established on the roots.

The association of roots and fungi is a well-known symbiosis called a mycorrhiza. A great many, and perhaps most, plants growing under natural conditions have some type of mycorrhiza. The fungus assists the green plant in absorbing nitrogen and phosphorus and in return receives some of the plant's surplus carbohydrates. Members of the heath family commonly possess mycorrhizae, and the nitrogen-absorbing properties of the fungus may explain how heaths, heathers, and blueberries manage to survive on acid soils that are extremely low in nutrients.

Just when people had adjusted to *Monotropa* being a saprophyte instead of a parasite, Erik Bjorkman of the Royal School of Forestry in Stockholm pointed out that *Boletus,* the fungus, was not capable of breaking down cellulose but relied on dissolved glucose already present in the soil. Furthermore, there was simply not enough glucose in the soil at one time to account for the rapid growth of either Indian pipe or pinesap. According to Bjorkman, the enigma was quite simply stated: "How can a plant possessing no nutritional store of its own and no possibility of producing one, grow so rapidly during late summer (northern Europe) that, from insignificant underground germs, it reaches its full development in a week or so?"

Bjorkman noted that the fungus forming mycorrhizae on the roots of *Monotropa* was similar to the fungus forming mycorrhizae on the roots of forest trees and, in an insightful moment, asked whether the two might be parts of the same fungus and whether the *Monotropa* might be dependent on the trees after all.

To see whether there was a connection between pinesap and surrounding trees, he isolated clumps of pinesap by placing cylinders of sheet metal around them and driving the metal barriers deep into the ground, severing any connections between the pinesap and the living roots. The next year he watched for regrowth and was delighted to find that only a few weak stems emerged from the isolated clumps. Undisturbed clumps, by comparison, produced the usual number of normal stems.

To check further, he injected pines and spruces with glucose that was labeled with radioactive carbon 14 as a tracer. Four to five days later he examined the stems of pinesap growing a few feet away and found they continued the radioactive glucose. While there is no direct connection between *Monotropa* roots and tree roots, the fungus serves as a nutrient bridge by which carbohydrates pass from the tree to the growing *Monotropa*.

Suddenly *Monotropa* could no longer be considered a saprophyte. Instead it was returned to the category of a parasite. But information spreads slowly outside of technical journals. Bjorkman's findings were published in 1960 (*Physiologia Plantarum,* vol. 13, pp. 308–27), but many wildflower books still describe *Monotropa* as a saprophyte.

The Indian pipe and the pinesap are not saprophytes, but are they really parasites? It would be delightful to claim that they are. Gardeners are so familiar with plants getting a fungus that it would be most refreshing to learn of a fungus that suffered by getting a plant.

To be strictly considered a parasite, the *Monotropa* should be the only partner benefiting from the association with the fungus, but subsequent research has shown that when radioactive phosphorus is injected into Indian pipes, some of it winds up in neighboring maple, oak, and hemlock trees. Apparently there is two-way traffic on the nutrient bridge. Furthermore, the *Monotropa* produces chemicals that have a powerful stimulating effect on the growth of the fungus. With further study, the relationship will undoubtedly prove to lie somewhere between absolute parasitism and a fifty-fifty split of benefits.

Among woodland wildflowers, *Monotropa* is unusual in not using sunlight as an energy source. The Indian pipe and the pinesap grow and bloom beneath photosynthesizing hosts, species that are capable of forming mycorrhizae with the same fungus that surrounds the roots of the *Monotropa*. Although both the tree and the fungus benefit from the association that forms, the tree can live without the fungus and the fungus without the tree. However, the *Monotropa* can absorb neither energy from the sun nor nutrient from the soil. The waxy stalks with their delicate nodding bells are entirely dependent on the fungus connection.

The Ripening of a Tomato

Armed only with a pinch of salt, in her private game preserve the home gardener hunts the most elusive quarry—a tomato that is perfectly ripe. She searches among the foliage for a crimson globe that threatens to pull itself from the vine. For the taste of a sun-warmed, ripe tomato—plucked, seasoned, and eaten at once—is reward enough for the five months of attention the plants have received. But even as she eats the soft pulp, reveling in the fragrant, ripe tomato taste, a cloud cuts off the sun, and the cold September wind blows a reminder that these tender tropical plants from the western foothills of the Andes will soon be frosted.

To rescue the tomatoes that have not yet ripened, she will pick them green, lining them up on her kitchen windowsill, wrapping them in newspaper in a bureau drawer, or hanging them from whole vines suspended in the basement. There they will slowly ripen, providing fresh tomatoes while leaves fall and the garden is prepared for winter.

Every garden manual contains instructions for ripening tomatoes indoors, but will they taste as good as the spontaneous salad she has just finished eating? The answer, unfortunately, is no. Recent investigations into tomato flavor have explained why the insipid, pale pink golf balls sold in supermarkets taste so bad. The simple explanation, of course, is that they were picked green. Even the most obstinate proponent of commercial tomatoes will acknowledge that his tomatoes would taste better if they were allowed to ripen fully on the vine. He shrugs his shoulders as he does so, explaining that there is no way a ripe tomato can be shipped without arriving as catsup. Commercial growers such as the California Fresh Market Tomato Advisory Board are sensitive to criticism leveled at their product. They wince when Craig Claiborne of the *New York Times* declares store-bought tomatoes to be "tasteless, hideous, repulsive." And, in response, they and others have supported considerable research on how a tomato achieves its taste.

The tomato begins life even before the flower opens. It is an unusual fruit because cell division is virtually complete by the time the flower is pollinated. This period of cell division is followed by one of cell enlargement, until a full-sized, sour, hard, green fruit is produced. This is termed a mature tomato. In the garden this mature tomato then undergoes a gradual transition to palatability, a process we call ripening. It involves a complex of chemical changes.

The most obvious occurrence is a change in color. The

green disappears as the chlorophyll breaks down, and the fruit is left slightly whitish. Then two carotene pigments are synthesized, turning the fruit yellow. As a third pigment, a red one called lycopene, is produced, the fruit turns orange, orange red, and finally red.

As the tomato ripens it also softens. The insoluble calcium pectate binding the cells together is converted to soluble pectin. That soft succulence of a ripe tomato results from the adjacent cells separating easily when the flesh is bitten into.

While color and texture are important aspects of ripeness, flavor is determined by the sugars, organic acids, and volatile chemical compounds present in the fruit. As the tomato turns from green to red the sugar content rises and the organic acid content falls. The tomato described as being "low acid" by a taster may in fact be high in acid, the acid being masked by the sugar. Claims in advertisements that a tomato is low in acid because it tastes that way have no factual basis. To date, 118 volatile chemical compounds have been identified in the ripe tomato. These chemical compounds evaporate readily, resulting in an aroma. Since the taste buds detect only sweetness, sourness, saltiness, and bitterness, the flavor of a tomato, as with other foods, is perceived through the nose. Synthesized as the tomato ripens, the relative abundances of these volatile chemical compounds control the variation in flavor.

This elaborately choreographed chemical ballet, with its series of appearances and exits, is the tomato fruit's last performance. The proceeds, in the form of a highly edible fruit, then will be used to promote seed dispersal.

Unlike the above tomatoes, those sold in supermarkets

have been picked mature green and gassed with ethylene to trigger their ripening. The gas cannot be blamed for their subsequent poor quality because ethylene is produced naturally when the fruits are allowed to ripen themselves. Much of the extreme criticism of commercial tomatoes is rightfully directed at fruit which have been picked before they reached the mature green stage, at a time when the seeds could still be cut if the fruit were sliced open with a knife. Such a tomato may turn appropriately red, but the flavor at best will turn from bitter to tasteless. If the tomato has been picked at the proper green stage, ripened and stored under optimum temperatures, the ripened fruit will have some of the familiar flavor of a real tomato. But recent studies at the University of California have shown that even these fruit have a lower level of sugar, less vitamin C, and an off-flavor attributable to a different balance of volatile chemical compounds.

This information applies to the home gardener as well. Only some of the green tomatoes she takes inside will have reached the mature green stage; the others will be immature. Regardless of which method she uses to ripen green tomatoes, they will never achieve full flavor. She may be proud of the tomatoes she ripens for Thanksgiving or even Christmas, but their quality will be little better than the commercial tomatoes denounced as insipid. The really ripe tomato with its wonderous taste is indeed an elusive quarry, to be pursued avidly during those few weeks each year that it is in season.

The Cultured Cabbage

*Few and signally blessed
are those whom Jupiter has destined
to be cabbage-planters.*

FRANÇOIS RABELAIS

When confronted by rows of full-grown cabbages, I feel more overwhelmed than blessed. Whether I have planted 'Early Jersey Wakefield' or 'Premium Late Flat Dutch,' the results are the same. From 62 to 110 days after the seeds are sown, the cabbage is ready to pick, an enormous poundage—or even tonnage—that has all matured at once. It would be nice to be able just to admire the rows of heavy heads with their spreading, blue-green outer leaves, but the cabbages won't stop growing. As the younger leaves curled up inside the head grow larger, the outer leaves cannot stand the pressure from within and the head splits open. Exposed to sunlight, some of the inner leaves turn green, while others that have been separated from the core by the splitting begin to rot. Cutting the roots on one side of a cabbage plant by thrusting a shovel into the ground near the stem will delay the splitting of a head, but it only postpones the inevitable. Eventually something has to be done with the cabbage.

Our family once tried to eat an entire cabbage crop fresh, with the result that our house rivaled a local restaurant in the amount of coleslaw served. When no one could eat coleslaw any longer, we switched to stuffed cabbage, then to boiled cabbage, and then to cabbage soup. Dollops of sour cream laced with caraway seeds prolonged our taste for cabbage soup, but eventually it too became unwelcome. Cabbage has a very distinctive flavor, and whether you mix it with tomatoes, ham, cheese, or even chestnuts, the taste of the cabbage is still perceptible.

We talked of planting different kinds of cabbage to spread out the harvest, but instead we ended up making sauerkraut, "a clean, sound product, of characteristic flavor, obtained by full fermentation, chiefly lactic, of properly prepared and shredded cabbage in the presence of not less than two percent nor more than three percent salt." The characteristic flavor of sauerkraut is no more subtle than that of cabbage, but at least you don't have to eat it all at once. What the federal government's definition fails to mention is that sauerkraut is also the easiest and cheapest way to store cabbage and that its popularity was no doubt originally due more to the product's keeping ability than its taste.

Laborers building the Great Wall of China in the third century B.C. were fed boiled rice and cabbage during the summer. In the winter they were fed boiled rice and pickled cabbage, the cabbage having been preserved in vinegar. The Korean dish *kimchi* is apparently a direct descendant of this dish. The Great Wall didn't stop Mongols from invading China, and among their booty was the recipe for pickled cabbage. When they ultimately reached Europe, they carried the recipe with them. Somewhere in Eastern Europe it was discovered that shredded cabbage would ferment naturally, without adding vinegar, provided it was lightly salted, and the Austrians named this new dish sauerkraut. Recipes for pickled cabbage that involve adding vinegar are thus not merely quick substitutes for the real thing, but an approximation of the earliest preserved cabbage. Naturally fermented sauerkraut is comparatively modern.

The popularity of sauerkraut in Europe grew until Alexandre Dumas commented that while the surest way to get yourself murdered in Italy was to question the beauty of the women, or in England to question the freedom of the people, the surest way to get killed in Germany was to doubt that sauerkraut was food for the gods.

Sauerkraut was more than a tart accompaniment to heavy foods like sausage, pork, and goose. It was an important source of vitamin C when fresh fruit and vegetables were scarce. The Dutch sailors ate *zuurkool* on voyages, and in 1772 James Lind, an English surgeon, noted that unlike their British counterparts, the Dutch sailors were not contracting scurvy after months at sea. To combat this dread disease, the British prescribed sauerkraut for the navy in 1780 and subsequently for sailors in the merchant marine. Only later was sauerkraut replaced by limes, a more concentrated source of vitamin C. It is amusing to speculate that if the British sailors had continued to rely on sauerkraut, they might have become "krauts" instead of "limeys."

German and Dutch immigrants brought sauerkraut to the United States where it became a staple dish. When

Robert E. Lee captured Chambersburg, he ordered twenty-five barrels of "saur-kraut" for his victorious Confederate troops, and sauerkraut has garnished millions of Nathan's hot dogs on Coney Island.

Sauerkraut's long history, however, is not enough to interest some people in making it, even when they are faced with an overabundance of cabbage. They say they don't like its taste. This antipathy toward sauerkraut isn't a recent occurrence. An observer in 1656 noted that the cabbage "they pouder up" in Russia "stinks most grievously." A pamphlet on the profitable cultivation of cabbages in the United States written in 1895 claimed that "sauerkraut is by no means, if rightly made and prepared for the table, the vulgar, appetite-turning article of diet that prejudice has made it," but the authors themselves sounded unconvinced. Today those who disdain sauerkraut can claim the company of such gourmet luminaries as Raymond Sokolov, food critic and writer, who calls it a mash suitable only for stuffing turkey in the Serbian dish *podvarak*.

While no food can be expected to inspire unanimous approval, such a wide range of opinions seems unusual. How can sauerkraut at once be considered food for the gods and, as one wit put it, a form of silage (unless of course god is a cow)? The explanation is that there are many different kinds of sauerkraut. The single word *sauerkraut* no more describes the range of flavors in fermented cabbage than the word *wine* describes the subtle differences in fermented grape juice or *cheese* the array of curdled milk products. Although kinds differ greatly in delectability, there is no popular terminology to differentiate one sauerkraut from another. Like the child who, after one bite of spinach, announces he doesn't like vegetables, many Americans who have tasted it once assert that they don't like sauerkraut.

Microorganisms are responsible for the taste of sauerkraut, and the final flavor depends on which ones are involved. In cheese making, the curd is often inoculated with a specific organism, such as *Penicillium roqueforti* or *Penicillium camemberti,* but in making sauerkraut no inoculation is required. The bacteria needed to ferment the cabbage are already present. Successful fermentation, however, depends on preventing the growth of other molds, yeasts, and bacteria. These, if given the chance, would turn the fresh cabbage into a putrid mass, with an odor resembling the untreated effluent of a paper mill.

To flavor the growth of only certain bacteria, the right environment must be provided. A 2.5 percent concentration of salt not only inhibits the growth of many spoilage organisms, but seems to promote the growth of a bacterium called *Leuconostoc mesenteroides.* In an anaerobic brine at temperatures of sixty-five to seventy-five degrees Fahrenheit (eighteen to twenty-four degrees Celsius), the bacteria increase in numbers, consuming the sugar present in the cabbage and synthesizing lactic acid, which further protects the cabbage against spoilage. *Leuconostoc mesenteroides* also produces carbon dioxide, acetic acid, ethanol, mannitol, dextran, and esters, all of which contribute to the flavor.

Once the lactic acid content in the brine reaches one percent, the *Leuconostoc mesenteroides* is replaced by two additional lactic-acid-producing bacteria, *Lactobacillus plantarum* and *Lactobacillus brevis*. These continue to produce acid, and provided there is sufficient sugar present, the acid content may reach 2.4 percent. Ordinarily, however, it levels off at 1.7 percent, yielding a sauerkraut that is light colored and crisp, with a clean, acid flavor.

Most tasters would find such sauerkraut delicious, but there are lots of other sauerkrauts. If, for example, the temperature is ninety degrees Fahrenheit (thirty-two degrees Celsius) or the salt content in the cabbage is 3.5 percent, then the growth of *Pediococcus cerevisiae* is encouraged, resulting in a highly acid sauerkraut that is generally considered inferior. If, in addition to extra salt, air is allowed to reach the fermenting cabbage, then red yeasts will grow producing a pink kraut. Air and high temperatures may result in brown or black kraut.

Some of these alternative forms of sauerkraut are universally unpopular; slimy or ropy kraut, for example, which is caused by certain strains of *Lactobacillus,* is considered unsalable. On the other hand, some people prefer the cheesy flavor of sauerkraut that has had surface yeast growing on it following regular fermentation.

The variation in sauerkraut flavor is no secret to commercial manufacturers. Since the founding of the National Kraut Packers Association in 1907, there have been sauerkraut "cuttings," similar to wine tastings, where different samples of sauerkraut are tasted at once. The average palate seems to prefer a mild-flavored sauerkraut, one that blends well with other foods without imparting a strong flavor. Such sauerkraut has been made into ice cream and added to recipes for chocolate cake. Sauerkraut juice mixed with tomato juice and flavored with lemon and horseradish is popular as an eye-opener.

If the natural variation in sauerkraut flavor is not enough, various seasonings can be added to the shredded cabbage before it ferments. Juniper berries and caraway seeds are the most common, but one Hungarian recipe calls for sliced quinces, horseradish, black peppercorns, caraway seeds, tarragon leaves, and dill.

One unpleasant experience is no reason to give up sauerkraut altogether. Cabbage planters should not hesitate to make their own. A wooden barrel was once used for the purpose, but the tannins in the wood darkened the sauerkraut. Glazed clay crocks are better, but older ones tend to leak. We like the five-gallon plastic pails that bakeries will sell after emptying them of cake icing or prune Danish filling.

The cabbage is harvested, the outer leaves stripped off, and the heads rinsed in cold water. Slicing the cabbage into thin strips is time consuming, but it is more or less so depending on the method. In Budapest, buyers of cabbage once hired mustachioed sauerkraut slicers to follow them home and slice their cabbage for them. Hand slicing soon gave way to a simple machine, which in Germany was called a *kohlhobel*, or cabbage plane. In this country one can buy a flat board with a series of adjustable blades over which the cabbage is slid. Owners of food processors will have an even easier time.

For every five pounds of sliced cabbage, three tablespoons of pure (noniodized) granulated salt should be thoroughly mixed in. Then the cabbage should be tightly packed into the container, eliminating any air pockets. (Strict traditionalists will want to do this wearing a clean pair of wooden shoes.) The salt will draw moisture out of the cabbage, creating a brine that covers the cabbage when it is pressed down. To hold the cabbage submerged, a plate or board weighted down by a rock was once used, but this permitted air to reach the brine and promoted the growth of mold. A great improvement is the use of a heavy plastic bag, like those sold for freezing turkeys, partly filled with water and placed on top of the cabbage. The weight of the water keeps the cabbage pressed down, while the bag spreads to seal off the brine from the air, still allowing bubbles of carbon dioxide to escape.

The hotter it is, the faster the cabbage ferments, but although sauerkraut is ready in eight to ten days at ninety degrees Fahrenheit, it is a poor product. In the fall temperatures are more likely to be around seventy degrees (twenty-one degrees Celsius), and in the dark at this temperature a delicious sauerkraut develops in two or three weeks. If you are late getting started, cabbage will still ferment at forty-five degrees (seven degrees Celsius), but it may take six months or more.

Once bubbles have stopped forming, the sauerkraut has finished fermenting. Don't be talked into canning it; this merely defeats its purpose. Fermentation is a natural means of preservation, and as long as the sauerkraut is kept cool, it will keep for many months.

By keeping the batches small, there is no risk of disaster. Should one batch not suit your taste, you can give it away to someone whose taste differs. The kind of cabbage, the amount of salt, the temperature, and other intangibles will conspire to affect each vintage. Like wine or cheese making, the fermentation of cabbage is a gracious art. I've never understood why Mark Twain claimed that a college-educated cabbage was a cauliflower when clearly a cultured cabbage is sauerkraut.

The Squirrel
and the Fruitcake

Pecans are a choice ingredient of both fruitcakes and squirrels. Some ten million pounds are incorporated annually into each. In fruitcakes, pecans improve the color, texture, and taste, for the nuts offset the darkness, gumminess, and molasses flavor of the candied fruit. In squirrels, the nuts are vital. A diet of pecans, with their 70 percent oil content, is responsible for a higher birthrate, increased survival of the young, reduced emigration, and longer life for adults. In short, more squirrels.

With the quality of both squirrels and fruitcakes dependent on the seeds of *Carya illinoinensis,* there has always been competition for the nuts.

From the point of view of the nut grower, squirrels make off with far too many pecans. Climbing into the trees, the squirrels begin to feed on the nuts even before they are ripe and later remove the largest and finest nuts from the opening shucks. Nuts that have fallen are picked up off the ground. In all, a single squirrel may make off with fifty pounds of pecans in a four-month period. Some of these nuts are eaten on the spot; others are carried up to a hundred feet away and cached singly in shallow holes dug in the ground.

From the squirrel's point of view, the human is far too successful at usurping the harvest. Nut trees that have been planted far away from adjoining forest are often surrounded by a dangerous expanse of closely mown ground; crossing this open ground means exposure to hawks, foxes, dogs, and other squirrel eaters. Reaching the grove may provide little sanctuary: guns and traps baited with pecans constitute another, greater hazard. If someone has protected the trees with eighteen-inch-wide bands of aluminum flashing tied around the trunks, the trees are unclimbable anyway. Scarcely any nuts are on the ground until they are knocked or shaken from the trees by the harvesters, and when that happens the grove is filled with people. For a squirrel whose ancestors harvested pecans long before humans appeared on this continent, this is an unpleasant development.

The displeasure that humans and squirrels may share at having to divide up the pecan crop is compounded by the periodic disappearance of pecans from a tree altogether. The nonproduction of nuts is a periodic occurrence, especially in the year following a heavy harvest. A heavy crop will exhaust the tree's supply of stored carbohydrates, and the ripening of so many nuts prevents the tree from storing enough carbohydrates to bear the following year. Pecan growers refer to this as "alternate bearing" and determinedly try to prevent it through breeding, high fertilization, and careful spacing and pruning of trees to promote additional photosynthesis. As a further strategy, growers often plant four or five pecan cultivars in a single grove so that some of the trees will be bearing each year.

While growers and squirrels may both consider a year without pecans to be a crop failure, from the point of view of the pecan tree itself, such a year is not a failure at all. Pecans are reproductive units intended to increase the population of pecan trees, not squirrels. A given pecan tree might fruit every year, but then there would always be the same number of squirrels, pecan fed and ready to consume all of the crop once again. On the other hand, a pecan tree that saved up its carbohydrates for several years would not be feeding squirrels. There might be fewer squirrels in the absence of pecans, and when the tree did fruit, producing a much larger crop because of its stores of carbohydrates, the reduced squirrel population might be unable to consume all of the nuts. Some pecans would escape to become pecan trees.

For a pecan tree to effectively elude nut predators by concentrating its nut production into one year, all the trees in the vicinity must bear nuts the same year. Otherwise the predators will simply feed on the nuts of one tree one year and the nuts of another the next. This synchronization is not as improbable as it sounds. There already exists remarkable synchronization among nut trees, even in forests containing many species. Measurements on the amount of hickory nuts, acorns, beechnuts, and other seeds in a forest in southeastern Ohio from year to year showed a range of 35 to 220 pounds per acre.

Whether in a forest or a grove, the concentration of nut production into only a few years results in lean years, which to both squirrels and pecan growers are entirely unwelcome. But from the point of view of the pecan tree, nonproduction means that the tree is not losing its nuts to predators. The pecan tree can't give up fruiting altogether, because eventually the tree must reproduce itself. The tree has simply evolved a specific behavior, in the form of irregular fruiting, that serves at least partially to prevent the total destruction of the nut crop by squirrels and other predators.

Ecologists and evolutionary biologists term this behavior "predator satiation." There are some extremely dramatic examples among plants. The bamboo *Phyllostachys bambusoides,* for example, fruits only every 120 years, with all the plants doing so at once. Among nut trees the interval is much less, usually a year or two between seed crops, but the bitternut *(Carya cordiformis)* has a three-to-five-year interval and the white oak *(Quercus alba)* a four-to-ten-year interval. The European beech *(Fagus sylvatica)* accumulates starch in the parenchyma of the sapwood for about eight years. It is then virtually completely incorporated into a single seed crop and then storage is resumed.

While the pecan trees have evolved a way to assure the survival of some of their nuts, they also have become dependent on squirrels to distribute and plant those same nuts. The thickness of the shell of wild pecans is largely a result of selection by squirrels. Pecans whose shells are too thick or too hard to be pierced by squirrel teeth will not be collected, and the trees producing these nuts will remain unpropagated. Pecans whose shells are too thin are likely to be eaten much too readily rather than buried in the ground where a small percentage will remain to germinate.

With the arrival of modern agriculture, the pecan is no longer dependent on the squirrel for propagation. Seedlings are grown in nurseries and transplanted into groves. Careful breeding and improved cultural practices have greatly improved the pecan tree. New cultivars bear early, annually, and prolifically. Nuts are larger, have thinner shells, and are well filled. The only situation that hasn't improved is the problem with squirrels.

The annual loss of pecans to squirrels is difficult to compute. In Georgia alone, an estimated ten million pounds of pecans are eaten by predators, including crows, blackbirds, and jays as well as squirrels. If we assume that squirrels account for one-third of this amount and, further, that Georgia produces roughly one-third of the nation's pecans, then we arrive at an annual nationwide loss to squirrels of ten million pounds of pecans a year.

Boxcar figures are not very useful and indeed they tend to obscure the much greater losses experienced by certain pecan growers. Especially in years of a small harvest, the loss may amount to more than 50 percent. In such "short crop" years, every nut on a tree may be stolen. One expert remarked sardonically that, in some areas of Georgia, pecans are borderline between a cash crop and wildlife feed.

Some people, especially those who have just lost a sizable portion of their pecan crop, would be in favor of exterminating squirrels. Because attempts to exterminate them would almost certainly fail, current efforts are focused on reducing the numbers of squirrels by hunting and trapping or keeping them away with noisemakers, metal barriers around trunks, or fine-wire fences reinforced with electricity.

From what we have learned of the behavior of squirrels and pecan trees, an alternative squirrel-control method suggests itself. Since we have undertaken to improve the pecan tree through artificial breeding and selection, why not produce a squirrel-proof pecan? Whether or not the effort of selecting for squirrel resistance is economically feasible remains to be determined, but such a cultivar is certainly possible. This hypothetical squirrel-proof pecan cultivar would have the following two characteristics, traits the opposite of those being favored by current selection practices.

1. The cultivar would fruit only after long intervals of time, five to ten years if possible, with little or no nut production in intervening years. With all the adjoining trees fruiting at the same time, there would be a single enormous crop that would satiate squirrels and other predators.

2. Nuts of the cultivar would have a very thick shell, too thick for squirrels to gnaw through easily. If the costs in energy of breaking into a nut exceed the nutritive value of the nutmeat therein, the squirrels will turn to other foods. Thicker-shelled pecans would prompt squirrels to seek more accessible nutrition.

Groves of this new pecan should still be isolated from other food sources of squirrels to make it difficult for squirrels to move into a fruiting grove. Home gardeners who might have to plant these trees close to an adjoining squirrel habitat would probably benefit more from the thicker-shelled feature than from the concentrated bearing. On the other hand, concentrated bearing would offer both the home gardener and the commercial grower considerable relief from such insect pests as the pecan weevil and the hickory shuckworm. These pecan pests are much more dependent on pecans for survival and their populations will crash more dramatically than squirrels in the nonbearing years.

A number of objections to squirrel-proof pecans come immediately to mind and must be addressed. Will pecan trees that fruit only once a decade mean nine years of nutless fruitcakes? Absolutely not. Different parts of the country could be on different schedules with one grove bearing this year, another the next. It would only be necessary to establish nut-free zones between unsynchronized groves of pecans. A second solution is to store pecans between harvests. Fifty years ago pecan storage had not progressed beyond that achieved by squirrels. Pecans could be kept fresh during the cool winter months, but as soon as spring warmth arrived, the nuts became stale and rancid. Since then, however, it has been shown that in controlled cold storage, pecans can be kept for eight years with no loss in color, flavor, or texture of the shelled pecans. A long hiatus between harvests will deprive only the squirrels, not the fruitcakes.

A second objection will come from fanciers of papershelled pecans, those nuts that are easily shelled by hand. However, less than 10 percent of the pecan crop each year is sold to consumers in the shell. The remaining 90 percent is machine shelled. There is no reason why the established cultivars could not continue to provide nuts for the in-shell market. The new thicker-shelled cultivar would simply require a stronger machine.

Finally, conservationists concerned about preserving the squirrel population need not be alarmed. Squirrels have sufficient quantities of food available to them in the form of a host of wild edibles that they face no danger of extinction.

This highly hypothetical proposal for a squirrel-proof pecan is illustrative of a different approach to crop plant design. In breeding plants to conform to our commercial needs, we tend to ignore their peculiar characteristics, traits that have evolved during centuries of selective pressure, in this case the fruiting cycles of nut trees. More efforts should be directed at reexamining the biology of wild crop plants for clues to their natural resistance to pests and disease. In some instances we may have overlooked a trait, and in the process of artificial selection, we may have exacerbated a problem rather than alleviated it. Domestication of plants has removed some ecological constraints, such as a need for natural propagation. In seeking means to meet existing pressures, we may be able to select more vigorously for a certain trait than previous ecological constraints would allow. Most trees fruit more often than once a century because there is too much danger of their being blown down or burned up before they reproduce. Having undertaken to propagate pecan trees ourselves, we can select for longer rather than shorter intervals between harvests and for nuts with heavier shells. This may ultimately prove to be an easier way to reduce nut losses than trying to exterminate the predators. With new pecan cultivars, we could have our fruitcake and squirrels, too.

Rotten Apples

The orchard is bare, the vineyard a tangle of leafless vines, and the vegetable patch offers nothing but parsnips. The year's harvest has been taken indoors and put away—essential provisions for the approaching months when fresh fruits and vegetables will be scarce. As the first snow flurries whiten the meadow, it is comforting to survey the fruit room, the cold cellar, the attic, replete with canned goods, root crops, apples, dried beans, and squash.

It will be many months before rhubarb and asparagus usher in a new season, and some of the stored produce will rot before it can be eaten. Although rot is an age-old problem, centuries of experimentation, accidental and intentional, have yielded ways to reduce spoilage, ranging from the old-fashioned drying and pickling to the more modern canning and freezing. The most effective methods are often too expensive or alter the flavor of the food too much, so apples still turn brown, dried onions go soft, carrots get black spots, and butternut squash occasionally dissolve. If men were bears, we could avoid all these difficulties by eating everything at once, storing it safely as fat, digesting it as needed during the winter. But men are not bears.

In the struggle to protect his cache of winter food, man has been mostly unaware of what causes food to rot. Microbes were first identified as a cause of spoilage when Louis Pasteur, after studying failures in wine and beer production, proclaimed in 1857 that microorganisms were responsible for fermentation, an economically beneficial form of spoilage. Subsequently, a host of microscopic fungi and bacteria have been identified, each responsible for a distinct form of rot. Plant pathologists have discovered fifty genera that cause rot in apples in the United States alone. Their common names represent a kaleidoscope of decay: pink rot, blue rot, gray, brown, and black rot. Further study of the postharvest physiology of fruits has sought to explain why ripe fruits are so likely to rot. The results indicate that ripe fruit has a much lower resistance to infection than green fruit. While the fruit is green there are chemicals present that prevent microbes from multiplying, but when the fruit ripens, these disappear, because their presence would probably make the fruit less palatable to a seed-dispersing animal. Thus the very deliciousness of a ripe fruit means that it is more likely to spoil.

Whether it is a rotten apple or moldy sauerkraut, man has a strong aversion to eating spoiled food; and with good reason, for many of the fungi and bacteria produce extremely toxic chemicals as they metabolize the food they are infecting. Most cases of food poisoning are the result of eating spoiled food. Botulism and salmonella poisoning are well-known examples of toxic bacteria, though there are infamous fungi as well. Ergot is produced when rye grain is infected by *Claviceps purpurea*. When grain infected with this fungus was made into bread, whole villages became stricken with St. Anthony's Fire, an often fatal affliction. According to some authorities, the incidences of satanic possession leading up to the Salem witch trials were scattered cases of ergot poisoning. Species of *Aspergillus*, another grain-infecting fungus, produce aflatoxins that are among the most potently carcinogenic substances known.

The role of these toxic chemicals in the life of the microbes was not at first clear. But in 1928, Alexander Fleming found that colonies of the bacteria *Staphylococcus aureus* were killed by secretions of the fungus *Penicillium notatum*, a discovery that resulted in the antibiotic penicillin. On a broader scale, his discovery led to the recognition that in any spoiling food, whether a ripe fruit or a sack of grain, microbes are waging war with one another for possession of the resource, using the toxic chemicals as weapons.

What has been proposed only recently is that the microbe-produced chemicals may also serve to prevent large animals from usurping the food supply. An apple is nutritious to both man and microbe. If, shortly after a fungus invades a McIntosh apple, the apple is eaten, then the fungus has lost its food resource, has been deprived of its chance to reproduce, and has possibly lost its life as well. On the other hand, if the invading fungus can quickly render the fruit unpalatable, then the fungus can grow and reproduce at leisure. The approach is the same as that of a child presented with a plate of cookies, who quickly licks each one to guarantee that no one else will eat them before he has a chance. If the toxins are poisonous enough to make an animal (or person) sick when it eats infected food, but not so poisonous as to kill it outright, then the animal will learn not to eat spoiled food.

Daniel Janzen, the ecologist from the University of Pennsylvania who proposed this idea, cites two examples of rotting apples. *Penicillium expansum* causes soft rot or blue mold in apples, the principal cause of storage losses in the United States. Bite into the soft, watery, yellow-textured portion of an infected apple and you will discard the apple at once because of its unpleasant moldy taste. The fungus has just won. This fungus produces a toxic chemical called patulin or clavacin, poisonous to man and animals and of concern in the cider industry in instances where infected fruit is pressed. *Sclerotinia fructigena* is another fungus, this time a cause of brown rot, a major cause of storage loss of European apples. The rot is accompanied by the production of methanol in the fruit. Most vertebrates will not eat alcoholic fruit. Anecdotal accounts of animals that do, however, indicate that they become tipsy, a condition making them more likely to be preyed upon or to injure themselves.

So the next time you sort through the apples in your root cellar and discard a rotten one, don't think of the loss of the apple as a failure to keep up with simple deterioration. Recognize that a complex and well-equipped microbe has just beaten you to the draw.

White Life

The vegetable garden disappeared last night. It is out there somewhere, on a line between the apple tree and the telephone pole, but trying to locate it would mean trudging through knee-deep snow. A heavy snowfall like this, the first of the winter, cuts off the supply of kale and brussels sprouts and may confine people indoors for a short time, but it is at the same time a sort of liberation. The outdoor projects that didn't get done, now can't be done, and there is no longer any reason to feel guilty about putting the work off. It's too late to bring the stacked bean poles into the barn, to sow winter rye as a cover crop, or to do a final weeding. Knowing that you can't do these things is nearly as satisfying as having done them.

Snowfall not only provides a general amnesty for procrastinators, but does an excellent job of whitewashing the facts. If you didn't gather up your dead tomato and squash vines, your neighbor will never know. Overnight the wreckage of a bygone growing season disappears and all gardens become equal. Some writers use the words "blanket of snow" to describe new snowfall, but blankets can't even hide wrinkles in a sheet, let alone cabbage stumps. A better term for snowfall, with its accompanying freedom from further gardening responsibility, would be "comforter of snow."

"Think Snow" command the bumper stickers on half the passing cars. With nothing pending in the garden, now is the time to do it. Think Snow, but not of the hard-packed surface on which to slide strips of wood, plastic, or metal. Think Snow, but not of the metaphorical substance used by poets to signify frigidity, isolation, and death. Think Snow, and this time think of snow's life-giving and life-supporting properties. Think of it as insulation, as a refuge, as a place to live, and as a source of water and nutrients.

With air trapped between each hexagonal crystal, snow provides excellent insulation. Beneath a few feet of it, the ground may be seventy Fahrenheit degrees (forty Celsius degrees) warmer than the air. The daily fluctuations in air temperature do not penetrate snow, and the cycle of freezing and thawing does not exist. When deep snow comes early, there is no need to mulch perennial plants, for the snow will prevent their heaving and protect their dormant crowns.

Eskimos once built snow houses when traveling or wintering on sea ice to hunt seals. Today mountaineers occasionally spend the night in snow caves. During a blizzard, cottontail rabbits will allow themselves to become buried, waiting until the weather improves. Ruffed grouse and ptarmigan will burrow into snowbanks on cold nights.

Snow also insulates the territory of mice and voles, whose networks of narrow runways lead through the matted grass beneath the snow. It may not be excessively cold in these rodent passageways, but it is damp and dark, for two feet of snow filters out all but about 4 percent of the sunlight. The moisture and dampness promote decay. Spurred on by a late application of lawn fertilizer and unfrozen soil, several types of snow mold may spread across the buried grass, resulting in dead patches when the snow melts in the spring. Carbon dioxide, the by-product of decay and animal respiration, tends to accumulate beneath the snow, pooling in hollows. To escape this toxin, voles dig ventilation shafts to the surface, but the air issuing from these round openings is a signal to foxes. With stiff-legged leaps into the snow, the foxes seize their prey and reduce the damage these rodents cause to the roots and bark of fruit trees.

Unlike grouse, rabbits, or foxes, snow insects are too small to leave tracks in the snow. Yet on a warm spring day when the snow has melted away from tree trunks and rocks, thousands of snow fleas may appear on the snow surface. These tiny black collembolans possess a forked appendage that can be folded beneath the abdomen and triggered suddenly, causing the quarter-inch insects to spring four inches into the air.

Snow fleas are harmless, even to snowmen. They ordinarily live in leaf litter and feed on microorganisms and other products of decay. Why they should appear on the surface of the snow, sometimes in unbelievable numbers, remains completely unknown.

Equally mysterious is the appearance of several species

of *Boreus,* flightless scorpion flies about twice the size of snow fleas. These may appear at any time during the winter on warm days, jumping about on the surface of the snow. A third, less common insect is the snow fly, or thick-legged gnat. This species of *Chionea* is one of the crane flies but looks much more like a spider than a fly. Walking awkwardly about on the snow, these wingless insects are apparently searching for mates.

The most impressive invertebrate found in the snow is the snow worm. On snowfields and glaciers in California, Oregon, Washington, and Alaska, these inch-long black worms have been seen massed over more than forty acres of snow. Sometimes called glacier worms, these segmented worms of the genus *Mesenchytraeus* are capable of boring through hard-packed snow at will and appear on the surface at certain times of day. Some of them are consumed by birds; some find their way into drinks served in Yukon bars.

Where snowfields melt in summer the snow worms spend part of their life in the soil, but on permanent snowfields and glaciers they spend their entire life surrounded by snow. To survive, these unusual annelids have come to rely on an equally unusual food—snow algae. Algae, some of which have evolved to live in the warmest hot springs, have also evolved to live on the coldest glaciers.

Aristotle was the first to mention colored snow, but John Ross was among the first to collect any—from an eight-mile stretch of red snow cliff overlooking Baffin Bay in 1818. It was not until the late nineteenth century that biologists were able to explain the phenomenon: dense populations of colored algae on the snow surface. Although individual algae are only one micron to one hundred microns in diameter, high concentrations, or "blooms," containing up to 500,000 algae per milliliter of snow, can occur, and the result is snow tinted red, orange, or green, depending on the species of algae involved. Green snow occurs where there is shade, red snow in full sun, and orange snow under intermediate conditions. To date, more than one hundred species of snow algae have been identified in the world. While some of these are not restricted to snow, others are true cryophiles (cold lovers) and grow only at temperatures close to freezing.

Even snow algae cannot grow when the snow is frozen; there must be a supply of melted water. Thus, in the mountains of North America where snow algae are most conspicuous, the algae do not usually appear until May or June. They may first be apparent in the tracks of alpine hikers, red footprints caused by compacting the snow and increasing the density of algae.

It is intriguing to wonder how the algae colonize a new snowbank in early spring. While it is possible that in some cases spores are carried by wind from snow-free soil or that birds carry algae in their guts or on their bodies, in the case of *Chlamydomonas nivalis,* the algae move to the surface of the new snow. Experiments at Oregon State University have shown that these algae lie dormant beneath snow during the winter and in the spring produce flagellated cells that swim up through the snow to the surface where they begin to multiply.

The snow worms feed on the snow algae, and the algae in turn feed on snow—at least partially. Sunlight, water, and carbon dioxide are necessary for algal growth, but essential nutrients come from the snow. (Even without algae and worms and ptarmigan, snow is not nearly as sterile as poets would have you believe.) Snowbanks contain nitrates, phosphates, and a host of other organic and inorganic compounds. Some of these come from contact with soil, others from debris blown onto the soil surface. But even new-blown snow isn't pure water; it contains the atmospheric nuclei around which the snowflakes first crystallized.

On permanent snowfields, the nutrients in snow cycle through a food chain that includes algae and snow worms, but on the vegetable garden the warm winds of spring will return these nutrients to the soil. Snow is the poor man's fertilizer. The same white drifts that protected dormant plants during the winter will yield essential moisture and nutrients for next summer's crops. The heavy flakes drifting down on a gray December afternoon may signal the end of one growing season, but just as certainly they bring promise of another.

Mistletoe

Over the doorway someone has tucked a sprig of mistletoe into a spray of white pine and holly. Turning from the fire to get more punch, a young man is startled under the lintel by a woman who throws her arms about his neck and kisses him solidly, serving up a round of laughter to the guests.

It would be easiest to say that, like Yule logs and plum pudding, the tradition of kissing under the mistletoe originated with the English. Indeed it may have, but the roots of the mistletoe tradition go much deeper into history. Throughout Europe many scattered groups considered mistletoe *(Viscum album)* to be, among other things, divine, a fertility agent, a cure-all, a bestower of mystical powers, or a protection against witchcraft, lightning, and physical harm.

The Druids, ancient inhabitants of Gaul, Britain, and

Ireland, harvested mistletoe during the winter solstice for use in their religious ceremonies, selecting only the rare specimens that were growing on oak trees, because they believed the sacred oak contributed additional powers to the mistletoe. The Druids also hung mistletoe in their homes to attract the kind spirits from the forest, thus perhaps originating the use of mistletoe as a domestic decoration.

Norse folklore tells the story of Balder, son of Odin, whose mother, Frigga, sought to protect him by placing all earthly objects under oath not to harm her son. However, she overlooked the insignificant mistletoe growing west of Valhalla. The evil Loki fashioned a spear from mistletoe, and Balder was slain. Today, however, many Scandinavians hang mistletoe above their doorways to keep out evil spirits and wear finger rings made from it to ward off sickness.

The plant's parasitic habit may have been the source of the legends and beliefs surrounding it. Seeing that the mistletoe grew from the branches of trees without connection to the ground, men must have marveled that a plant could grow without drawing sustenance from the earth. In addition, the plant's ability to remain green and in leaf when the host plant has shed its leaves may have suggested immortality.

When European colonists first arrived in North America, they found a mistletoe that looked much like their own growing widespread in the forests. They identified this North American variety as *Viscum album* and transferred all their traditional significance to it. In actuality, this mistletoe, growing from New Jersey to Florida and west to Texas, is *Phoradendron serotinum,* a genus that does not occur in the Old World, but this distinction was not made until 1847.

Phoradendron serotinum, our familiar Christmas Cupid, is an evergreen parasite whose yellow green foliage appears in clumps up to three feet in diameter on branches of host trees. Some sixty-two species have been identified as hosts, ranging from the persimmon to the red maple and the black walnut. The flowers of this mistletoe are minute, with the two sexes on separate plants. On the female plant, the flowers give way to watery, translucent white berries that are harvested for Christmas decorations.

In the wild, the berries are eaten by winter birds, but the seed in each berry has a sticky coating that causes it to adhere to the beak or feet of the bird. To remove the seeds, the bird scrapes its beak against a tree trunk, thereby transporting the seed to a growing place. The seed soon germinates and sends out a root that forms an adhesive disk when it makes contact with the bark. From the underside of this disk is formed the haustorium, a specialized organ that parasitic plants use to obtain nutrition from the host plant. This haustorium grows into the cambium layer of the host tree and sends out so-called sinkers that grow until they contact the xylem vessels of the host. From the xylem the mistletoe obtains water and minerals. *Phoradendron serotinum* is considered a semiparasite, for it does not feed on the primary products of photosynthesis contained in the phloem of its host. The mistletoe has its own chlorophyll; it only relies on its host for water, minerals, and a place in the sun.

Phoradendron serotinum grows very slowly. The visible

shoot does not appear until the second year, and by the end of the third year it may only be one and one-half inches long. But once the haustoria and sinkers are firmly established, the plant grows rapidly, reaching full size in six to eight years.

There are at least seven hundred species of mistletoe in the world; some authorities would double that number. Formerly, all the mistletoes were grouped in one family, the Loranthaceae, but recently the family has been divided into two families, the Loranthaceae and the Viscaceae (which contains *Viscum* and *Phoradendron*). Most species of mistletoe are tropical or subtropical. Their host relationships can be ornate. For instance, there are mistletoes that parasitize other mistletoes, and there are even cases of hyperparasitism to the second degree, where one mistletoe is growing on another, which in turn is growing on another, which is growing on a host.

Perhaps the most spectacular mistletoe occurs on the other side of the world. *Nuytsia floribunda,* found only in southwestern Australia, is a tree twenty to forty feet high. The gray bark and the dark green leaves contrast sharply with the masses of yellow orange blossoms that appear in December. Although the tree is terrestrial and photosynthetic, the roots form haustoria around the roots of other plants growing in the surrounding savannah. These hosts range from grasses to *Banksia* and even cultivated carrots. A one-inch-thick underground electric cable was even found with a haustorium cutting through the insulation and shorting out the cable. While it is not clear how much this tree relies on its many hosts for nourishment, it is intriguing to find a full-size tree that is partly parasitic on the grasses growing around it.

The residents of southwestern Australia consider *Nuytsia floribunda* to be the most spectacular of their flowering trees and welcome its peak of bloom at the end of December. Here, in spite of temperatures in excess of one hundred degrees Fahrenheit (thirty-eight degrees Celsius), they celebrate Christmas with roast beef, Yorkshire pudding, and a rousing game of tennis. There is no Yuletide snow, but there is *Nuytsia floribunda* with its flaming masses of flowers, and they call it their Christmas tree.

Ex Familia

In February 1448, Ludovico Gonzaga sent his wife a little box of melon seeds and told her to plant them wherever she wished in the vineyard. In March he wrote and told her where to find the hazelnuts he had saved and asked her to sow two kinds. Ludovico, a condottiere-prince and ruler of the Italian city-state of Mantua, was required to spend much of his time away from home, attending to negotiations or military campaigns. But he never ceased to be concerned about details of planting and harvesting along the broad, fertile floodplain of the Po River. In his forty-five years of marriage to Barbara of Brandenburg, he continually wrote home, sending her as many as four letters a day. These letters, along with her replies—thousands of small pieces of paper neatly lettered in quattrocento script—were tucked away in the vaults of the family castle in Mantua. They have survived Austrian and French invasions, though cartloads of other papers were burned in the streets, and today they reside in a state archive, the most detailed and complete family correspondence remaining from fifteenth-century Europe.

I can't read these letters myself—the language is midway between Latin and Italian and full of regional idioms—but I am about to marry a woman who can recount the hopes, the anxieties, and the daily news of Ludovico and Barbara as though she rode to work with them on the bus. Renaissance Italian history is a recondite interest for most people, but studying the daily life of people who died five hundred years ago seems quite natural for Elisabeth. Whether we are drinking wine and watching pigeons circle the cathedral in Florence, or back in Boston watching oarsmen skim the Charles, the conversation often turns to families. Tracing the influence of one generation on another, or outlining the complex interplay of inspiration and obligation that accompanies long and productive marriages, she moves freely across cultures and centuries. One is left with an expansive feeling of security, increasingly aware of the multiple possibilities that are characteristic of family life.

But what can a connoisseur of families and an admirer of duckweed have in common? After all, Renaissance history and science writing are seldom mentioned in the same breath. Yet on the eve of our marriage, it occurs to me that our interests are remarkably parallel, a more serious explanation for our compatibility. Elisabeth studies family history, looking for, discovering, and reporting events of daily life. While other historians are studying diplomacy and government, military campaigns, and great ideas, Elisabeth collects data on how babies were weaned, how children were taught, what people ate, and what they did for fun.

With Elisabeth studying the history of the family, I find that I am writing about what I call the science of the familiar, which concerns common objects, everyday events, things too ordinary to elicit any special comment. The two words—*family* and *familiar*—have the same Latin root meaning household, and in a sense both of us derive our information *ex familia,* or from the household. Just as Elisabeth doesn't study the formation of democratic institutions, I seldom write about the origin of the universe or gene splicing, nuclear accidents or the medical effects of zero gravity. Instead my articles are about rotten apples and woodchucks. But even the most unspectacular roadside weed has an evolutionary history and is probably symbiotic with a pollinating insect. The secondary chemical compounds in the plant's tissues not only protect it from enemies, but also may have therapeutic properties in human medicine. The plant's distribution reflects the movements of glaciers and men.

Why emphasize the familiar? There are many good justifications. One could point out that every major scientific discovery is based on countless smaller, often quixotic, investigations, or that the secrets of life are contained in a buttercup. These would be justification enough, but there is an even more compelling reason. By closely examining familiar events, daily life is enriched. Knowing how honeybees perceive a flower or how tomatoes ripen means that whenever we encounter bees or tomatoes we are reminded of the information, and both the bees and the tomatoes are suddenly much more interesting. By comparison, we are unlikely ever to encounter a black hole, or at least have any chance to appreciate it. The familiar is always present. To achieve an increased awareness, an increased appreciation of common events, is to discover the exotic in our own backyard.

Exploring the science of the familiar also brings a sense of optimism about the future, for in the elaborateness of life one soon perceives a resiliency. At present there is a widespread belief that because everything is interconnected, our careless destruction of a portion of the world will shortly and inexorably destroy the rest. But a look at the diversity of life, both in terms of species and the different pathways one species can take, gives strong evidence that the world will survive. There are different bacteria in sauerkraut, different duckweeds in ponds, and different barks on trees. Life is accustomed to periodic disasters. When the chestnut blight struck, some feared that great holes might forever be left in our forests. Not surprisingly, the oaks moved in rapidly to fill them. Life is just as well equipped to handle the disasters inflicted on it during this period of ignorant and tumultuous misuse of our environment. Life comes in enough shapes and with enough skills to tolerate our youthful excesses. When we have learned to be less rambunctious, the world will be waiting, ready for a more mature companionship.

Reading the correspondence of Ludovico and Barbara has caused Elisabeth to come to the same conclusion about families. There is enough diversity among them, enough different ways of raising children successfully, that we need not fear the disintegration of families just because things are changing rapidly today. I have the same confidence about the rest of the world. It is an optimistic outlook, one blended from facts and faith, and it seems a good time to get married.

Further Reading

TIME, ENERGY, AND MAPLE SYRUP

PERRIN, N. *The Amateur Sugar Maker*. Hanover, N.H.: University Press of New England, 1972.

NEARING, H. and S. *The Maple Sugar Book*. New York: Schocken, 1950.

WALTERS, R. S., and Shigo, A. L. "Tapholes in Sugar Maples: What Happens in the Tree." Forest Service General Technical Report NE-47, Northeastern Forest Experiment Station, Broomall, Pa., 1978.

STEINHART, J. S. and C. E., "Energy Use in the U.S. Food System." *Science* 184:4134(1974):307–16.

GUSSOW, J. D. *The Feeding Web: Issues in Nutritional Ecology*. Palo Alto, Calif.: Bull Publishing, 1978.

A TASTE FOR PARSNIPS

BLEASDALE, J. K. A. "Space to Grow." In *Know and Grow Vegetables* by P. J. Salter *et al*. Oxford: Oxford University Press, 1979.

BOSWELL, V. R. "Changes in Quality and Chemical Composition of Parsnips Under Various Storage Conditions." University of Maryland Agricultural Experiment Station, Bulletin No. 258, 1923.

OF COWS AND COWSLIPS

WHITTAKER, R. H. "New Concepts of Kingdoms of Organisms." *Science* 163:3863(1969):150–60.
MARGULIS, L. "Symbiosis and Evolution." *Scientific American* 225:2(1971):48–57.

SEED TRAVELS

VAN DER PIJL, L. *Principles of Dispersal in Higher Plants.* New York: Springer-Verlag, 1972.
KLEINFELDT, S. E. "Ant-Gardens: The Interaction of *Codonanthe crassifolia* (Gesneriaceae) and *Crematogaster longispina* (Formicidae)." *Ecology* 59:3(1978):449–56.
HANDEL, S. N. "The Competitive Relationship of Three Woodland Sedges and Its Bearing on the Evolution of Ant-Dispersal of *Carex pedunculata.*" *Evolution* 32:1(1978):151–63.

SKOTOTROPISM: A SHADY BEHAVIOR

STRONG, D. R., JR., and Ray, T. S., Jr. "Host Tree Location Behavior of a Tropical Vine *(Monstera gigantea)." Science* 190:4216(1975):804–6.
RAY, T. S., JR. "Slow-Motion World of Plant 'Behavior' Visible in Rain Forest." *Smithsonian* 9:12(1979):121–30.

SALTING THE EARTH

MCCONNELL, H. *et al.* "De-Icing Salts and the Environment." Habitat School of Environment, Belmont, Mass., 1972.
POLJAKOFF-MAYBER, A. and Gale, J., eds. *Plants in Saline Environments.* New York: Springer-Verlag, 1975.

THE EDUCATION OF A WOODCHUCK

SETON, E. T. "The Woodchuck." In *Lives of Game Animals.* Garden City, N. Y.: Doubleday, Doran and Co., 1928.

SCHOONMAKER, W. J. *The World of the Woodchuck.* Philadelphia: J. B. Lippincott, 1966.

DUNG HO!

HEINRICH, B., and Bartholomew, G. A. "The Ecology of the African Dung Beetle." *Scientific American* 241:5(1979):146–56.

WATERHOUSE, D. F. "The Biological Control of Dung." *Scientific American* 230:4(1974):100–109.

TAIGANIDES, E. P., ed. *Animal Wastes.* London: Applied Science, 1977.

THE ATTRACTION OF WILD BEES

SEELEY, T. D., and Morse, R. A. "The Nest of the Honey Bee *(Apis mellifera L.)*." *Insectes Sociaux* 23:4(1976):495–512.

SEELEY, T. D. "Measurement of Nest Cavity Volume by the Honey Bee *(Apis mellifera)."* *Behavioral Ecology and Sociobiology* 2:2(1977):201–27.

MORSE, R. A., and Seeley, T. D. "Bait Hives." *Gleanings in Bee Culture* May 1978:218–20.

DUCKWEED

Making Aquatic Weeds Useful: Some Perspectives for the Developing Countries. Washington, D.C.: National Academy of Sciences, 1976.

HILLMAN, W. S., and Culley, D. D., Jr. "The Uses of Duckweed." *American Scientist* 66:4 (1978):442–51.

ZEUS AND THE ASH TREE

VIEMEISTER, P. E. *The Lightning Book.* Cambridge, Mass.: MIT Press, 1972.

IN THE NIGHT GARDEN

PROCTOR, M., and Yeo, P. *The Pollination of Flowers.* London: Collins, 1973.

ROEDER, K. D. "Moths and Ultrasound." *Scientific American* 212:4(1965):94–102.

LLOYD, J. E. "Studies on the Flash Communication in *Photinus* Fireflies." Miscellaneous Publications, Museum of Zoology, University of Michigan, No. 130, 1966.

THE FUNGUS CONNECTION

BJORKMAN, E. "*Monotropa Hypopitys* L.—An Epiparasite on Tree Roots." *Physiologia Plantarum* 13 (1960):308–27.

FURMAN, T. E., and Trappe, J. M. "Phylogeny and Ecology of Mycotrophic Achlorophyllous Angiosperms." *Quarterly Review of Biology* 46:3(1971):219–25.

THE RIPENING OF A TOMATO

KHUDAIRI, A. K. "The Ripening of Tomatoes." *American Scientist* 60:6(1972):696–707.

WHITESIDE, T. "Tomatoes." *The New Yorker* 24 January 1977:36–61.

RICK, C. M. "The Tomato." *Scientific American* 239:2(1978): 76–87.

THE CULTURED CABBAGE

FRAZIER, W. C., and Westhoff, D. C. *Food Microbiology.* 3rd ed. New York: McGraw-Hill, 1978.

PEDERSON, C. S., and Albury, M. N. "The Sauerkraut Fermentation." State Agriculture Experiment Station, Geneva, N.Y., Cornell University, Bulletin No. 824, 1969.

THE SQUIRREL AND THE FRUITCAKE

BARKALOW, F. S., JR., and Shorten, M. *The World of the Gray Squirrel*. Philadelphia: J. B. Lippincott, 1973.

NIXON, C. M., McClain, M. W., and Donohoe, R. W. "Effects of Hunting and Mast Crops on a Squirrel Population." *Journal of Wildlife Management* 39:1(1975):1–25.

JAYNES, R. A., ed. *Nut Tree Culture in North America*. Hamden, Conn.: Northern Nut Growers Association, 1979.

WOODROOF, J. G. *Tree Nuts*. 2nd ed. Westport, Conn.: AVI, 1979.

ROTTEN APPLES

JANZEN, D. "Why Fruits Rot, Seeds Mold, and Meat Spoils." *American Naturalist* 111:980(1977):691–713.

JANZEN, D. "Why Food Rots." *Natural History* 88:6(1979): 60–65.

WHITE LIFE

PALMER, E. L. "The Snow Blanket." *Natural History* 70:1(1961):35–46.

POLLOCK, R. "What Colors the Mountain Snow." *Sierra Club Bulletin* 55:4(1970):18–20.

HARDY, J. T., and Curl, H., Jr. "The Candy-Colored, Snow-Flaked, Alpine Biome." *Natural History* 81:9(1972):74–78.

MISTLETOE

KUIJT, J. *The Biology of Parasitic Flowering Plants*. Berkeley, Calif.: University of California Press, 1969.

Index